Diana

Diana

A Portrait in Her Own Words

EDITED BY BILL ADLER

William Morrow and Company, Inc.
New York

It is the policy of William Morrow and Company, Inc., and its imprints
and affiliates, recognizing the importance of preserving what has been
written, to print the books we publish on acid-free paper, and we exert
our best efforts to that end.

Library of Congress Cataloging-in-Publication Data

Diana, Princess of Wales, 1961–1997
Diana : a portrait in her own words / edited by Bill Adler.—1st ed.
p.   cm.
ISBN 0-688-17003-X (alk. paper)
1. Diana, Princess of Wales, 1961–1997 Quotations.
2. Princesses—Great Britain—Biography Quotations, maxims, etc.
I. Adler, Bill.   II. Title.
DA591.A45D531334   1999
941.085'092—dc21
[B]   99-15270
CIP

Printed in the United States of America

First Edition

1   2   3   4   5   6   7   8   9   10

BOOK DESIGN BY DESIGN 2000

www.williammorrow.com

Contents

Acknowledgment	vii
Introduction	1
Chronology	3
Childhood	9
Courtship	15
The Wedding	22
Married Life	28
William and Harry	40
Public Life—	
"The Things I Do for England!"	56
Good Works	82
Children	119
The Media	129
Fashion	142
The Royal Family	146
Affairs	153
Squidgygate	160

Contents / vi

Christie's Auction   165

Miscellaneous   168

The Final Days   177

Acknowledgment

Many thanks to Tom Steele for his creative assistance.

Introduction

To the entire world, she seemed born to be a princess. The endless reach of her charisma, her effortless glamour, and her eventual, unprecedented candor utterly transformed our notions of royalty—forever.

By the time her spectacular wedding was held, the words "fairy tale" were regularly used everywhere to describe the event. At her wrenchingly premature funeral, it seemed that the whole planet ground to a halt.

Between these two seismic events lived the most beloved royal presence of our century, and one that was surely as multifaceted as any present-day celebrity. The radical twists and turns in her brief life drew the fascination of millions. For surely no figure in our time has been the subject of more printed words in just sixteen years of public life than Princess Diana.

Yet the most photographed woman in history

was also the most seldom quoted. Indeed, other than her famous BBC *Panorama* interview in 1995, her actual words were rarely heard, and never gathered. Until now.

A scrupulous search for every significant recorded word has resulted in this book, the only collection of her revelatory remarks and insights that takes you through her magical and tragic life.

Behind the headlines, behind the highborn pedigree, behind the "Shy Di" veneer dwelled a woman of extraordinary resourcefulness, stamina, and—perhaps above all—excruciating vulnerability. Today, her frankness about the events and people around her is both disarming and startling.

Take her at her word—her *own* words—and discover the astonishing clarity, endless warmth, and surprising wit that she brought to her legendary life. This is an intimate self-portrait of the woman who became "the People's Princess."

This is the closest we will ever get to an autobiography.

Chronology

July 1, 1961: Lady Diana Frances Spencer is born.

❧

1967: Diana's mother leaves her husband and her four children.

❧

1969: After a bitter, two-year divorce trial, Diana's father receives custody of the children. (Her mother's own mother testifies against her daughter's character.)

❧

1976: Diana's father marries Countess Raine Dartmouth, daughter of romance novelist Barbara Cartland.

❧

Summer 1980: Diana and Prince Charles finally "connect" and begin a courtship.

❀

February 24, 1981: Charles and Diana announce their engagement on television in their first public appearance together.

❀

July 29, 1981: 750 million people tune in to "the wedding of the century."

❀

June 21, 1982: Birth of Prince William

❀

September 15, 1984: Birth of Prince Harry

❀

June 1992: Andrew Morton's book, *Diana, Her True Story,* says that Diana tried to kill herself five times because of jealousy and her difficult marriage.

✣

August 25, 1992: The London *Sun* publishes a fairly lurid transcript of a New Year's Eve 1989 telephone conversation between James Gilbey and Diana (referred to as "Squidgy" by Gilbey, hence the term "Squidgygate").

✣

December 9, 1992: Prime Minister John Major announces that Charles and Diana are separating "amicably."

✣

January 14, 1993: Tabloid newspapers publish a transcript of a lewd conversation between Charles and his old friend and mistress, Camilla Parker Bowles.

✣

December 3, 1993: Diana announces that she is withdrawing from public life.

✣

June 29, 1994: In an interview, Charles says he was unfaithful to Diana after their marriage broke down.

※

August 1994: Newspaper reports claim that Diana had been making hundreds of annoyance calls to her friend Oliver Hoare, and hanging up when his wife answered the phone. She denies it.

※

October 3, 1994: Anna Pasternak's book, *Princess in Love,* claims that Diana had a five-year affair with British Army Major James Hewitt, her former riding instructor. She reportedly denies the allegation.

※

March 3, 1995: Camilla Parker Bowles and her husband, Andrew, divorce.

※

August 1995: Newspapers report a romantic link between Diana and Will Carling, captain of the

English national rugby team. Carling and his wife, Julia, announce separation on September 29.

❧

November 20, 1995: BBC broadcasts Diana's first solo television interview, in which she admits her affair with Hewitt, excoriates the royal family, questions Charles's fitness to be king, and says she does not want to divorce.

❧

November 24, 1995: Buckingham Palace announces that Diana will spend Christmas with them at Sandringham Estate.

❧

December 18, 1995: The Palace announces that Diana has changed her mind and made private Christmas plans, but that William and Harry will join their father.

❧

December 20, 1995: Queen Elizabeth urges the Prince and Princess to divorce.

❦

February 28, 1996: Diana announces she has agreed to divorce.

❦

January 13, 1997: Diana visits Angola with the Red Cross to decry the use of land mines.

❦

Summer 1997: Diana is romantically linked with millionaire Dodi al-Fayed, son of the man who bought Harrods of London.

❦

August 31, 1997: Diana and Dodi are killed in a violent car crash in Paris.

❦

September 6, 1997: Virtually the entire civilized world watches Diana's funeral, which is televised from Westminster Abbey.

Childhood

On her happy early childhood

"A lot of nice things happened to me when I was in nappies [diapers]."

꽃

Her favorite childhood home, Parker House, was "endlessly explorable, and filled with wonderful memories of so many pranks. I can see myself now, seated on the nursery floor, playing with my toys, totally into my own thing."

꽃

"I hated to be indoors [as a child]."

꽃

"My father said, 'Treat everybody as an individual and never throw your weight around.' I was brought up to look after others."

On her differences

"I always felt very detached from everyone else. I knew I was going somewhere different, that I was in the wrong shell."

🌿

"I was supposed to be a boy."

🌿

When her mother and father each gave her a new dress to wear at a cousin's wedding, she was rendered immobilized: "I can't remember which one I wore, but I remember being totally traumatized by it because it would show favoritism."

On her early ambitions

"I said to my father when I was thirteen, 'I know I'm going to marry someone in the public eye,' thinking more of being an ambassador's wife— not the top one. I always had this thing inside me that I was different. I didn't know why. I couldn't even talk about it, but in my mind it was there."

❧

She once wished to be a ballerina, but she grew too tall. "I rather overshot the mark," she said.

On school

Diana's memories of school were quite mixed. "There were a lot of tears, because I hated leaving home. But I've built up so much from it ... maybe not in the academic world. I love being outdoors, and I was captain of this and that, and I won endless cups for diving and swimming, which I adore. That's why I really enjoyed it, just having lots of friends."

❧

Discussing her time at West Heath private school in Sevenoaks, Kent, where she boarded from 1972–1977: "I was a St. Trinian's–style terror, often in trouble. In spite of what my headteachers thought, I did actually learn something, although you wouldn't have known so from my O-level results. My years at West Heath were certainly happy ones. I made many friends, who I often see. Perhaps now when future generations are handing out punishments for talking after lights out, pillow fights, or illegal food, they will be told to run six times round this hall."

⚜

Punishment for misbehavior at boarding school was running six times around the assembly hall or weeding the garden. "I became a great expert at weeding."

⚜

"I wasn't any good at anything at school; I just felt hopeless. A dropout."

On the volatile marriage of her parents

"The whole thing was very unstable. I remember my mother crying. Daddy never spoke to us about it. We could never ask questions. Too many nannies."

✻

The night her parents broke up was "just awful, awful."

✻

The divorce of parents is "a discovery no small child can bear."

On her sisters

"[My sisters] always seemed to be leaving me behind."

✻

She once told her nanny, Mary Clarke: "I can't wait to grow up and be like my sister Sarah. I can't wait to fall in love and get married and have lots of children. But I'll never marry unless I really love someone. If you're not really sure you love someone you might get divorced. I never want to be divorced."

On her father's second wife, Raine

The Spencer children loathed their father's lover, Raine, whom he married in 1976. "I couldn't bear Althorp [father's estate] anymore," Diana said. "A hard Raine was falling." The children also referred to her as "Acid Raine," and regularly chanted within earshot the nursery rhyme, "Rain, Rain, Go Away."

Courtship

When Charles recalled for the press how he'd noticed Diana as "an attractive sixteen-year-old," she
remarked, "I suppose it makes a nice little seg-
ment of history, but I think he barely noticed me
at all."

※

Charles reencountered Diana when she was nineteen, in the summer of 1980. Three years had
passed, and he noted, "No more puppy fat." She
blushed, and joked: "I'm just taller now. I've
stretched the puppy fat."

※

During that encounter, Diana mentioned how
touched she had been watching him on television
at the funeral of his beloved great-uncle, Lord
Louis Mountbatten. "You looked so sad when you
walked up the aisle at the funeral. It was the most

tragic thing I've ever seen. My heart bled for you when I watched it. I thought: It's wrong. You are lonely. You should be with somebody to look after you."

❧

On her age difference with Charles: "Never really thought about it."

❧

"Gee, he's thirty-two. I'm only nineteen. I never thought he'd ever look twice at me."

❧

"At the age of nineteen, you always think you're prepared for everything, and you think you have the knowledge of what's coming ahead. But although I was daunted at the prospect at the time, I felt I had the support of my husband-to-be."

❧

Charles was to marry an unabashed virgin: "I knew I had to keep myself tidy for what lay ahead."

✤

After a date with the Prince, she would tell her flatmates, "It's appalling the way they push him around," and "They work him too hard!"

✤

Riddles abounded during the courtship. Diana told a London Press Association reporter: "I'd like to marry soon. What woman doesn't want to marry eventually. Next year? Why not?" Then she retracted her statement the moment it appeared. "I never said anything about marriage. I am terribly worried about it. It's very upsetting."

✤

During their courtship, Diana was completely quiet about Charles. She told journalist Harry Arnold: "You know I cannot say anything about the Prince or my feelings for him. I am saying that off my own bat. No one has told me to stay quiet."

✤

She felt she could neither confirm nor deny whether Charles had proposed. "I can't say yes or no."

❧

Her demure response to Charles's proposal: "Yes, please."

❧

"[Marrying Charles] is what I wanted—it is what I want."

❧

"I know what I'm doing. I will be able to cope."

❧

At a press conference just after the engagement was announced, Diana averred: "With Prince Charles beside me, I cannot go wrong."

❧

At her first television interview she said, "I feel my role is supporting my husband whenever I can and always being behind him, encouraging him.

And also, most important, being a mother and a wife. And that's what I try to achieve."

❧

When asked what interests she shared with Charles, Diana answered, "All outdoor pursuits except riding."

❧

As a result of a childhood accident in which she fell from her pony and broke her arm, she never again wanted to find herself on horseback. She told one of her former flatmates: "I even prayed to God to give me the courage to ride again. I desperately wanted to please Charles, to be able to ride with him because I realized it was so important for him, for us. And yet I just couldn't relax. I don't know why. I just couldn't. Sometimes I would cry alone at night about it."

❧

While Diana and Charles were courting, she attended the Ludlow Races, where she encountered Camilla Parker Bowles. "I felt so vulnerable. It

was clear that I was the outsider in that friendship. Charles was much keener to talk to Camilla
than to me. He practically ignored me. I felt that,
throughout that whole time, Camilla was simply
sizing me up. When Charles finished racing, it was
Camilla he ran towards and started talking to. You
could tell by the way they were looking at each
other that something was going on."

❦

She asked a friend, "Why does he care more about
[Camilla] than he does about me? I'm the one he's
supposed to be marrying, for God's sake."

❦

In November 1980, the *Sunday Mirror* ran a story
alleging that Lady Diana had spent two secret
nights with Charles aboard the royal train, which
was used by members of the royal family for official business travel. Diana pleaded, "Please believe me. I've never been on that train. I have
never even seen it."

❦

She denied telling a newspaper that she'd spent the nights of the alleged train incident because she had a hangover. "I never get hangovers."

❦

The pressures of such a public courtship took their toll. "I cried like a baby to the four walls. I just couldn't cope with it."

❦

She begged her flatmates not to be shy after the wedding. "For God's sake ring me up. I'm going to need you."

❦

On the last night she spent in her flat, on the eve of the official announcement of her engagement, Chief Inspector Paul Officer told her: "This is the last night of freedom in your life, so make the most of it." She recalled: "Those words felt like a sword through my heart."

The Wedding

"Will you be watching the wedding?" Diana asked one man at a garden party honoring the Year of the Disabled Person. "Yes," he replied. And then, momentarily confused by the radiant princess-to-be, he asked, "Will you?" "No," she said with a laugh. "I'm in it."

❧

As the impending wedding was clearly becoming one of the most spectacular ceremonies in British history, jitters set in. "I think I am realizing now what it all means," Diana told a reporter just two weeks before the wedding, "and it's making me more and more scared."

❧

Diana told her guests at a Buckingham Palace garden party: "I'm going to videotape it [the wedding] so I'll be able to run back over the best bits and rub out the part where I say 'I will.' "

She was obsessed with losing weight before the wedding. "I'm not waddling up the aisle like a duck."

Watching the prewedding coverage on TV, she grew quite nervous. "Do I really have to go out in front of all these people?" she asked her seamstress.

Raine's mother, the eccentric romance novelist Dame Barbara Cartland, was not invited to the royal wedding. "Her false eyelashes look like two crows flying into the White Cliffs of Dover," Diana once remarked.

To a blind well-wisher, a few days before the wedding: "Do you want to feel my engagement ring? I'd better not lose it before Wednesday, or they won't know who I am."

※

To more well-wishers, the afternoon after Charles's "stag night" before the wedding: "If [Charles] comes past, ask him why he's looking so pale."

※

Had Charles been a great help in the recent months? "Marvelous, oh, a tower of strength. . . . I had to say that because [he's] sitting there."

※

Overcome by the pressures of the impending "wedding of the century," Diana, in tears, told her sister Jane: "All I want to do is marry Charles. I can't face all this . . . look at everyone . . . I can't go through with it."

※

"I've asked for one hymn, 'I Vow to Thee, My Country,' which has always been my favorite since school days." (The hymn was also played at her funeral.)

❧

"We had a wedding rehearsal yesterday. Everybody was fighting. I got my heels stuck in some grating in the cathedral and everybody said, 'Hurry up, Diana,' and I said, 'I can't. I'm stuck.' "

❧

"The night before the wedding, Diana told an interviewer she planned "to be tucked up in bed, I think, early night." Charles blurted, "Not allowed to see me anyway the night before." "We might quarrel," Diana rejoined.

❧

"[On the night before the wedding] all night people were sitting out on the steps singing 'Rule Britannia' and every kind of thing. It really was remarkable, and I found myself standing in the window with tears pouring down my face."

On the wedding crowds: "It's wonderful to see people's enthusiastic reaction. A mass of smiling faces. It's most rewarding and gives me a tremendous boost."

On the steps of the cathedral, she asked, "Is he here yet?"

During her vows, she confused the order of Charles's names (Charles Philip Arthur George), rather understandably: "I, Diana Frances, take thee, Philip Charles Arthur George..."

At the altar, Charles whispered to Diana, simply, "You look wonderful." "Wonderful for you," she replied.

"It was heaven, amazing, wonderful, though I was so nervous when I was walking up the aisle that I swore my knees would knock and make a noise."

🌿

"After all this fuss [of the wedding], I am sure we will live happily ever after."

Married Life

Diana termed the early 1980s "my early fairy period."

✤

At the honeymoon press conference, she was asked what she thought of married life. "Highly recommended," she replied.

✤

Asked by the press on her honeymoon if she'd cooked breakfast yet, she replied, "I don't eat breakfast."

✤

On the honeymoon ship, she happened upon a group of men wearing only towels around their waists. "It's all right. I'm a married woman now, aren't I?"

✻

"Do you know, I have never been happier."

✻

Oil billionaire Armand Hammer told Diana: "You know, I can't say no to the Prince, whatever he asks me to do. I have so much confidence in him that if he asked me to jump through that window there, I think I'd jump through." The Princess smiled and replied, "Well, I'd jump right after you!"

✻

In a letter to her former nanny, Mary Clarke, shortly after her marriage: "I do get annoyed at not being able to do my washing and general ironing. I know sister Sarah would adore that situation! . . . I might even have to learn to ride a horse, Mary, as it is the only time I will ever see my husband on his own. . . . I adore being married and having someone to devote my time to."

✻

Charles asked her if she'd ever read Rudyard Kipling's *Just So Stories*. "Just so *what?*" she asked.

❧

"I enjoy Danielle Steel's books, but my husband disapproves. He doesn't like me reading light novels."

❧

In 1985: "I see my role as supporting my husband whenever I can and always being behind him, encouraging him. It's most important being a mother and a wife—that's what I try to achieve. Whether I do is another thing, but I do try."

❧

In December 1985, Diana danced onstage at the Royal Opera House, to the surprise of the audience—and Charles, for whom the performance was a Christmas gift. After eight curtain calls, she turned to Wayne Sleep, who'd partnered her onstage, and said laughingly, "Beats the wedding."

❧

"We both liked people. We both liked country life. Both loved children, work in the cancer field, work in hospices."

🜍

By 1987: "Prince Charles loves [Highgrove] and it's my dream home now."

🜍

Later, her feelings reversed. Highgrove, where Camilla acted as hostess at dinners for Charles's close friends, was, for Diana, "a return to prison."

🜍

At a private party, she broke away from a group, saying, "I must go and find my husband. As usual, he's surrounded by women."

🜍

"I would trade places with you anytime," she told a humble homemaker.

🜍

"Just because I go out without my husband doesn't mean my marriage is on the rocks."

❦

"When we first got married, we were everyone's idea of the world's most perfect couple. Now they say we're leading separate lives. The next thing I'll read in some newspaper is that I've got a black lover. No, to make matters worse, I'll have a black Catholic lover."

❦

"The truth about our separate lives is very simple. My husband and I get around two thousand invitations to visit different places every six months. We couldn't possibly get to do many if we did them all altogether so we decide to accept as many as we can separately. This means we get to twice as many places and twice as many people. I don't get the vapors anymore. I think I'm coping much better now."

❦

"I know what is going on. I know what people are thinking. Inevitably we are going to be frequently apart. It's the nature of the job. We both do lots of jobs in different directions, but our marriage is very good, thank you very much. We don't see as much of each other as we should."

❧

As late as 1991, Diana was still involved in attempts to convince the world that her marriage was doing well. In a story that appeared in *Good Housekeeping,* Andrew Morton quoted Diana: "Don't worry about me, my marriage is fine.... People jump to conclusions so easily. It is so easy for people to judge my marriage, but they don't understand me or my husband. I am never going to get divorced and that's that. Whatever people may think and say, I am very happy, thank you very much."

❧

Responding to tabloid newspaper stories about all the time she spent apart from Charles: "I sometimes have my friends to lunch if my husband's out. We have people to dinner whenever we can, but my husband goes out to dinners where the wives aren't required, so we can't always find a date to suit both of us."

※

"There I was in floods of tears, just needing him. And I'm told I have to book an appointment— with my own husband."

※

To Charles's valet, Stephen Barry: "I don't know what to do, I feel so unhappy here. Charles doesn't understand me. He would prefer to be out shooting or stalking or riding or chatting with his mother rather than be with me. Can't he understand that I need him to look after me? I feel he's abandoned me. He just leaves me here all day. I hate it."

※

When Charles left her for yet another meal with his mother, she asked, "Why do you do this to me? Why can't we just have a meal alone together for a change?"

🌿

Charles offered to throw a grand ball to celebrate Diana's thirtieth birthday. "I would hope that my husband would know me well enough to know that I didn't like that sort of thing."

🌿

When Charles suggested that she should become better informed so that they could have more intelligent conversations, she retorted, "The whole world thinks I'm fine just as I am. That ought to be enough for you."

🌿

She once told Charles: "You look like a stiff. You embarrass me in front of my friends."

🌿

During her first pregnancy, she said, "I cannot tell you how bloody awful it is. They call it morning sickness. But I feel sick all the time."

꙳

After her second pregnancy was under way, she said, "I haven't felt well since day one. I don't think I'm made for the production line."

꙳

At a charity function in 1989, she told a dinner companion: "I want to have three more babies, but I haven't told my husband yet."

꙳

"My husband knows so much about rearing children that I've suggested he has the next one and I'll sit back and give advice."

꙳

"[Charles] ignores me everywhere and has done so for a long time."

꙳

She once told Charles: "The boys are entitled to happiness and see their father when they need him, not to be told he's running another meeting for the Crisis in Britain League. I need to get away from my royal duties, too; so do you."

✤

Diana discussed the 1994 Jonathan Dimbleby biography of Prince Charles with Peter Stothard, London *Times* editor: "Do you know that it originally was supposed to contain nothing about our relationship at all? How were readers supposed to think that the [children] came? By immaculate conception?"

✤

She told Charles: "My duty [as a mother] lies above my duty to you."

✤

The Palace insisted that Charles be at Diana's side after her father died, although she'd intended to leave Charles and their two boys behind. "Why are they bothering about him ignoring me now? He's been ignoring me for years already."

✤

In 1991, she still told most friends that Charles was "the same man today as on my wedding day."

✣

"However bloody you are feeling, you can put on the most amazing show of happiness."

✣

"My husband and I had to keep everything together because we didn't want to disappoint the public, and yet obviously there was a lot of anxiety going on within our four walls."

✣

"I think in any marriage, especially when you've had divorced parents like myself, you'd want to try even harder to make it work and you don't want to fall back into a pattern that you've seen happen in your own family. I desperately wanted it to work, I desperately loved my husband and I wanted to share everything together, and I thought that we were a very good team."

✣

When journalist Arthur Edwards asked her whether she intended to go watch Charles play polo, she replied, "No, I'm not going. I hate the game. I don't understand it and I never have. I also hate the sycophants who hang around it. So I'm not going at all this summer. The boys won't be going either. They don't like it and, anyway, it's a waste of quality time."

William and Harry

•

While touring Italy in 1985, Diana told Gianni Versace: "I miss my sons dreadfully. I love them so much, but in different ways. They are so very different. Speaking to them on the phone only makes me miss them more."

During her first pregnancy

"I hope it's a boy. But we'll have to wait and see."

❧

"Some days I feel terrible. Nobody told me I'd feel like this."

❧

Before William's birth, Diana adamantly told her physician, Dr. Pinker: "I shall of course be breast-feeding for as long as possible. I believe it is a very important part of bonding between mother and child."

❧

For more than the obvious reasons, Diana felt tremendous relief when William was at last born: "I felt the whole country was in labor with me."

❧

"Everybody was thrilled to bits. It had been quite a difficult pregnancy. I hadn't been very well throughout it, so by the time William arrived, it was a great relief."

❧

On her postpartum depression: "When I came out of the hospital I could barely put one foot in front of the other. My stitches were killing me. It was such a strain to stand there and smile even for just a few minutes. As soon as the car disappeared around the corner out of sight of the photographers, I burst into tears."

❧

Diana told a woman in the crowd waiting to see her in Nova Scotia: "I wish I had William with me. We've been away a few hours, but I miss him very much. I'm really sorry we couldn't bring him."

🌣

When William told the press that his greatest interest was "exploring wastepaper baskets," Diana whispered in his ear, "Who's the little superstar, then?"

🌣

On a visit to an orphanage, a thirteen-year-old asked Diana why William wasn't with her. "I didn't bring William today because he's a little pest. He won't do as he's told and touches everything." Then, while watching a seventeen-year-old demonstrate break dancing, she jokingly told him: "I'll buy you a new pair of trousers if you split those."

🌣

Diana vowed to protect her sons from frequent public duty for as long as possible. "My sons won't be pushed into doing anything public—unlike the Queen and Princess Margaret, who appeared in public at a very early age during the teens. William and Harry will definitely be broken in gently."

❧

"I just want my children to be happy and normal. I will do everything I can to help them achieve these very ordinary feelings."

❧

After Fergie [Sarah Ferguson] and Andrew's wedding in September 1986: "Did you see William? I'm glad he behaved himself because he can be a bit of a prankster. William is just like me, always in trouble, but he'll grow out of it."

❧

On choosing schools for the young princes: "I think it's too soon really. William's only three and

Harry one. And I think there's no hurry at all until we see what sort of characters they're going to produce as they get older, and then find a school that they can adapt to. Certainly, if William likes outdoor life we'll find a school that has that as its main feature."

❧

During their first official tour in 1983 to Australia, a young student asked Diana whether William had a favorite toy. "He loves his koala bear he's got, but he hasn't got anything particular. He just likes something with a bit of noise."

❧

Diana's favorite phrase at tucking-in time: "Who loves you most?"

❧

In the matter of her sons' nanny, Tiggy Legge-Bourke, who Diana felt was getting far too close to her sons *and* her husband, Diana said, "I am the boys' mother, thank you very much."

❧

"I am only too aware of the temptation of avoiding harsh reality, not just for myself but for my own children, too. Am I doing them a favor if I hide suffering and unpleasantness from them until the last possible minute? The last minute which I choose for them may be too late. I can only face them with a choice based on what I know. The rest is up to them."

❧

Talking to nurses at Marlow Hospital, where Prince William was taken after a classmate accidentally fractured his skull with a golf club: "It was a nasty wound which needed twenty-four stitches, but at least he's fine now, sitting up in bed at the Palace. I'm very relieved."

❧

"Only when the baby [Harry] is a lot older will he realize how lucky he is not being the eldest. The second child will never have the same sort of pressures or problems that poor William will always have to put up with."

🌿

"Prince William and Prince Harry can be little devils sometimes. But when they are, they get a whack where they can feel it. It's tiring work looking after children. I know because I have to look after my two boys and by Sunday I'm a stretcher case. But I love being with children and I miss them when they are not beside me."

🌿

During a visit with a young woman dying of cancer, the woman's mother told Diana that her son had pierced his navel. "God," Diana said, "if William ever did that, my mother-in-law would hit the roof."

🌿

On William: "He opens doors for women and calls men 'sir.' "

🌿

At a children's hospital in Surrey, she said, "William and Harry had lots of games for Christmas. I spent ages trying to work out how to play them by reading the instructions. But I found the instructions harder than the game. I'm as thick as a plank."

❦

On William's first day of school: "Well, I was [sad] because it's opening another chapter in my life, and certainly William's. But he's ready for it. He's a very independent child. He's surrounded by a tremendous amount of grown-ups, so his conversation's very forthright. He was so organized that day that he chose his shorts and shirt, and it's best to let him do that if you want him to smile at the cameras. . . . He was just so excited by it all, his first day of school, and there was a tremendous spirit of conversation. He was trying to get it all out. He just adored the children. He's very much an organizer which might be helpful in the future years; he really loved it. William's a typical three-year-old, enthusiastic about things. He's not at all shy, but very polite, extraordinarily enough, where perhaps Harry is quiet and just watches; he's certainly a different character."

❧

Comedian Joan Rivers remembers the day she met Diana. William had just gone off to Eton, and she asked Diana whether she'd redecorated his room yet. Diana replied: "I don't know whether to make it a sauna or a gym."

❧

"Sometimes [William] sounds like a thirty-year-old."

❧

"I want to bring them up with security. I hug my children to death and get into bed with them at night. I always feed them love and affection; it's so important."

❧

On William: "He's a deep thinker."

❧

"Charles and I have talked about how difficult their lives are going to be. We decided together to tell them everything before they read it or someone told them about it."

※

She told *Majesty* magazine's editor in chief, Ingrid Seward: "I have no wish to upset what is essentially part of William's inheritance, whether he likes it or not."

※

Her assessment of her sons in 1992: "William is a typical Gemini—very sensitive and emotional. Harry is a happy-go-lucky character who takes things in his stride. Harry is most at ease with the royal world. He loves castles and soldiers and pomp. William is very much his father's son in his sporting habits and is at his happiest at Balmoral."

※

"[William and Harry are] the only men in my life who haven't let me down."

꽃

On William at fourteen: "He's getting very tall—and we all know which side of the family that's come from."

꽃

"I found myself wanting to hug and kiss [my sons] all the time. But they have rather passed that stage. I kept reminding myself that they were nearly young men who didn't want to be kissed and hugged by their mother too much."

꽃

When Liz Tilberis, former editor of British *Vogue,* asked whether Diana had her kids with her, she replied, "Oh, no. They're in Scotland shooting little furry things with their father."

꽃

"I've told the boys, 'Remember there is always someone in a high-rise flat who doesn't want you to shoot Bambis.'"

☙

William saw headlines about his father that shrieked I NEVER LOVED HER. "Is it true, Mummy?" he asked. She replied, "When we first married we loved each other as much as I love you now."

☙

"I think it's important that they see the suffering in the world and have personal knowledge of it."

☙

"Both William and Harry, I take them around homelessness projects. I've taken William and Harry to people dying of AIDS, albeit I've told them it was cancer. I've taken the children to all sorts of areas where I'm not sure anyone of that age in this family has been before, and they have a knowledge. They may never use it, but the seed is there and I hope it will grow, because knowledge is power."

☙

"I want them to grow up knowing there are poor people as well as palaces."

❧

"I want them to experience what I already know— that they are growing up in a multiracial society in which not everyone is rich, has four holidays a year, speaks standard English, and has a Range Rover."

❧

On Harry learning about the world: "Through learning what I do and his father does, he has got an insight into what is coming his way. He's not hidden upstairs with the governess."

❧

In response to the suggestions that Princes William and Harry were too young to be introduced to homeless shelters and AIDS wards, Diana said, "I want them to have an understanding of people's emotions, of people's insecurities, of people's distress, of their hopes and dreams."

❧

What did Diana do on the weekends when Charles had custody of their sons? "I stay in town. If I go out, I keep my eyes down or straight ahead. Wherever I go, the press finds ways to spy, you know. Often I visit a hospice."

❧

"Harry is always asking me to have another baby because he is fed up with being the youngest. But I would have to marry someone who was prepared to cope with what I am."

❧

She felt she needed to explain to young Harry that the stunning beauties they saw in the area of Saint-Tropez were, in fact, transvestites. "He's thirteen going on twenty."

❧

Responding to criticism for taking her children with her to visit Fergie's former lover Paddy

McNally's villa in the south of France: "They are our children. They are not the possession of the Crown or State."

☙

Early in 1996, she told journalists: "The boys are both doing very well at school. William is doing well academically and doesn't really like it. He'd prefer to do other things but sticks to his work and is getting on fine."

☙

By May 1997: "William is six feet one inch now. The girls will love him when he is a little bit older. It's amazing that he is now taller than both his mother and his father."

☙

She frequently said, "The best part of my day is getting home to the children."

☙

Two months before she died, Diana said, "All my hopes are on William now. I don't want to push him. Charles suggested that he might go to Hong Kong for the handover, but he said, 'Mummy, must I? I just don't feel ready.' I try to din into him all the time about the media—the dangers, and how he must understand and handle it. I think it's too late for the rest of the family. But William—I think he has it. I think he understands. I'm hoping he'll grow up to be as smart about it as John Kennedy, Jr. I want William to be able to handle things as well as John does."

Public Life—
"The Things I Do for England!"

"My interests include a great interest in children and also ballet, but my interests will obviously be widened over the years. Many opportunities will arise and I look forward to considering these. I would very much like to help in any way in any areas I can. Obviously my life will be much busier and I look forward to that but I do hope we will also be able to have the opportunity to have some time to ourselves. As regards relaxation, I hope to continue with my dancing, swimming, and general outdoor activities. The interests [Charles and I] share are music, opera, outdoor sports, fishing, walking, polo. As regards the decoration of the homes at Highgrove and Kensington Palace, I have taken particular interest in the decorations but obviously have had to have advice."

❧

On life inside Buckingham Palace: "Not too bad.
But too many formal dinners (yuk!)."

On touring

During her first visit to Wales after her marriage,
she told Hywel Davies, the chancellor of St. David's Cathedral in Cardiff: "I didn't really believe
I was a princess until I stepped into Wales. Now
I know I am."

❧

Early on, she had a famous fit of giggles when
she met two kings, four princes, and eight princesses from the Jordanian, Greek, and Danish
royal families: "I was nervous, and when I'm nervous, I giggle. There were so many princes and
princesses there. It made me even more scared."

❧

Touring Italy in 1985, Diana virtually refused to eat most of what was put before her. "If I eat that, I will explode!" And when she saw the dozens of bottles of wine being served at one occasion, she blurted out: "All that? They drink all that?"

As the Italian tour wore on, she complained to her staff that she was "getting fed up with all this culture."

During the tour, when a British tourist congratulated Diana for being "a superb ambassador for Britain," she demurred (no doubt recalling the difficult early days of the journey), telling him: "Oh, I haven't done very well."

When Charles asked her what she remembered most about the Italian trip, Diana said, "The warmth of the people."

"Oh, you should have seen some of those Arabs going ga-ga when they saw me on the Gulf tour. I gave them the full treatment and they were all just falling over themselves. I just turned it on and mopped them up."

❦

On the assassination of Egyptian President Anwar Sadat: "He was just such a special man when he came to see us, and it was so sad because he was doing wonderful things in his country, and one minute he was there, the next minute he wasn't."

❦

Her hairdresser, Richard Dalton, remembers the time Diana and Charles were on the royal barge going down a canal in Venice, when she spotted a can of hairspray floating nearby. "Oh my God, Richard's fallen in," she said.

❦

During her meetings with her dress designers, David and Elizabeth Emanual, prior to her Gulf tour in November 1986, she explained: "It's a difficult one, this tour, because I have to hide my elbows, and have three-quarters-length hemlines. I think we might avoid the spots too! This tour is ten days to two weeks and we might be changing two or three times a day; it's a bit testing on the wardrobe. But I don't have to wear too many hats, so that's a relief."

❧

On the new prime minister, Tony Blair: "I think at last I will have someone who will know how to *use* me. He's told me he wants me to go on some missions. . . . I'd really, really like to go to China. I'm very good at sorting people's heads out."

On America

On Bill Clinton: "I find him rather dishy, and he *is* very tall."

❧

"When I was in Washington visiting the Reagans, whatever wasn't tied down they asked me to sign. I know Americans like you to sign things."

🌾

Her love of America and Americans was palpable. "When all the Americans come in July for Wimbledon, you can feel the energy go up. It all collapses again when they leave. Well, perhaps Tony Blair will change all that."

On speechmaking

At her first solo public appearance, to light the Christmas lights on Regent Street in 1981, she said simply, "I'm delighted to have this opportunity to make a small contribution to the Christmas spirit in London. I know these lights give a great deal of pleasure to countless people."

🌾

As she began to grow accustomed to public speaking, there were hurdles. "I just hate the sound of my own voice. I can't bear it. When I launched that new liner last week, I just couldn't believe it when I heard myself afterward. It just didn't sound like me."

※

"I just take out all the unnecessary words, flowery words—like wonderful and brilliant."

On celebrities

"It has been the greatest fun meeting a lot of the [rock and pop] groups. I like some pop music, but not all of it."

※

When John Travolta asked her to dance at the Reagan White House, Diana replied instantly, "I'd absolutely love to."

※

While dancing with Diana later that night, Clint Eastwood jokingly told her she was too old for him. She replied, "But I'm only twenty-four!"

❧

She told singer Meat Loaf that she'd attended a few of his London concerts. When he wondered why nobody told him, she said, "Well, we have ways of getting in."

❧

"We had a poster of the [dancers as] swans," said English National Ballet executive Richard Shaw, "and [Diana] said, 'Retake it with me in the middle. That will get you all the press you need.'"

❧

At a White House dinner, when Mikhail Baryshnikov got shy about customarily passing a menu card around the table to Diana for her autograph, she said, "Why? What's wrong? I have *your* autograph." Baryshnikov asked in a shocked tone: "What?" "As a teenager," she explained, "I stood in the rain outside the stage door at Covent Garden when you were dancing because I was such an admirer and I wanted your autograph."

🌺

At dinner with Luciano Pavarotti, he started to eat off her plate. "I'm not used to this," she said. Portraitist Nelson Shank, who was present, remembered the incident. "I don't think it bothered her at all."

🌺

Simon Le Bon, lead singer of Duran Duran, was taking a poster around for autographs at the Pavarotti and Friends concert for Bosnian children. Diana agreed to sign the poster, but said, "I'm not going to sign next to Duran Duran." LeBon asked, "Why not? You said we're your favorite band, and we've had to live with it." She replied, "I know I said it. I've had to live with it ever since as well." They both collapsed with laughter.

🌺

After actor John Hurt poked his rather tipsy head into the vehicle where Diana was chatting with a paraplegic in 1987, rather than being dismayed, she remarked: "Anything for a change of routine is fun. I love it when something unexpected happens."

❧

Fabled designer Oscar de la Renta was seated next to her at a charity luncheon. For the first half hour, Diana spoke with the lady next to her and never turned to him. A friend at a different table sent a note to de la Renta with the sarcastic comment, "We are all noticing what a hit you are with the Princess of Wales." Finally, Diana turned to him, took his hand, and said, "You know, I've wanted to talk to you for such a long time, but was too shy." He showed her the note, and she roared with laughter. She said, "Well, now we have to create a completely different impression." She spoke with no one but de la Renta for the rest of the meal.

❧

Upon entering a party at Cannes, she said to those gathered, "Sorry there aren't any film stars. There's just me. Hope you don't get bored."

※

Diana left this message for ABC-TV journalist Barbara Walters: "Just tell her it's Diana of London."

※

In February 1997, Diana saw an advance copy of Gianni Versace's *Rock and Royalty*, a coffeetable collection of photographs that included those of rock stars and other celebrities, some of them nude poses. She had written a foreword for the book. Diana quickly issued the following press release: "Last year I was approached by Mr. Versace to contribute a foreword to a book entitled *Rock and Royalty,* which was produced to raise funds for Elton John's AIDS Foundation. I had an interest in this Foundation and was pleased to support Mr. Versace's book. I was assured that the book would not contain material which would cause offense and I therefore signed the foreword. Earlier this

week I saw a copy for the first time. I am extremely concerned that the book may cause offense to members of the Royal Family. For this
reason I have asked for my foreword to be with-
drawn from the book and will now not attend the
dinner on February 18, which is intended to mark
the book's launch."

❧

When told by Jeremy Irons in 1995, "I've taken
a year off acting," Diana replied, "So have I."

On the public

"In a way, by being out in public [people] supported me, although they weren't aware just how
much healing they were giving me, and it carried
me through."

❧

In her first days of public life, on a crowded shopping street in Mayfair, someone called out: "Di!"

She replied, "Please don't call me that—I've *never* been called Di. I really don't like it."

※

A Q&A session with Grania Forbes of the London Press Association in July 1981 acquainted the public a bit better with their new princess: "I've been extremely touched by everyone's enthusiasm and affection. It has taken a bit of getting used to the cameras but it is wonderful to see people's enthusiastic reaction; it is most rewarding and gives me a tremendous boost. The Prince of Wales has made everything far easier for me and it is very good to be able to do things together publicly. I miss the immediate company of my flatmates. I'm enormously grateful to the many people helping so well with all the wedding arrangements and very much looking forward to visiting Wales and getting to know it better as part of my duties as future Princess of Wales."

※

A co-owner of the Young England Kindergarten remembers that, upon hearing that one of the teachers was engaged to a man named Charles King, Diana rejoined: "How funny that you are marrying Charles King, and I am married to the future King Charles."

❧

On fulfilling her first duties as a royal wife in Carmarthen, Wales: "The people who stood outside for hours and hours in the torrential rain. They were so welcoming. . . . I was terrified."

❧

To put an obviously nervous host at ease, she said, "I'd love a really black coffee. I went out with friends last night and I've got a bit of a hangover."

❧

At a polo tournament, she turned to a fellow spectator and said, "[Polo is] very boring, isn't it?"

❧

A stranger called out to her, asking: "May I kiss you?" "No," she replied, "but you can kiss my hand, though you never know where it may have been."

※

At one affair, she danced with various men, without apologies. "It's all so innocent, and I don't intend to act like the guilty party."

※

Responding to a letter from her friend Oliver Gilmour apologizing for several controversial remarks he made while conversing with Diana at the wedding of a mutual friend: "Oliver, I don't know what you're talking about. As you're so tall, it would have gone straight over my head anyway."

※

Stroking her host's dog at a dinner party, he remarked that he didn't think she liked dogs. "I don't like corgis," she replied, referring to her mother-in-law's famous brood of Welsh corgis. "They always get blamed for the farts."

On the difficulties and pressures brought about by public life

After her first official engagement: "What a long time to sit! I've got pins and needles in my bottom. I've never had pins and needles in my bottom before in my life!"

❧

"I am terrified that one day I might pop out of a low-cut evening dress and show everything. That would be too terrible for words. I would feel so terrible."

❧

Presenting awards for courage to ten youngsters at Westminster Abbey in 1985, she said, "I feel shy sometimes and still pretty nervous on big occasions."

❧

"Staying in the public eye is not worth the pain it's going to cause."

❧

One night she attended a gala concert, despite a bad cold. She later told the press: "Every time there was a quiet note, I'd go cough, cough, and you know when you're not supposed to cough, you cough more."

❧

She later remembered: "Anything good I ever did nobody ever said a thing, never said, 'Well done,' or 'Was it OK?' But if I tripped up, which invariably I did, because I was new at the game, a ton of bricks came down on me."

❧

"I was just pushed into the fire, but I have to say my upbringing was able to handle that. It wasn't as though I was picked out like *My Fair Lady* and told to get on with it. I did know how to react. When I first arrived on the scene I'd always put my head down. Now that I interpret it, it did look sulky. [But] I've never sulked. I've been terrified out of my tiny little mind."

❧

She later recalled her reaction to being suddenly addressed as "Your Royal Highness." "I was twenty years old, for goodness sake!"

❧

She told Dickie Arbiter, a journalist: "I certainly feel that since I've come into public life I perhaps need a little more guidance. I know that my grandmother has got all the answers, purely because she's been through some of the experiences herself, and it's so important to listen to someone older. We, the younger ones, always think we know better, but we don't—we have to go through experiences to learn the ups and downs of life, and it's an enormous help to have a grandparent around who will say it in the nicest way."

❧

"I felt compelled to perform—to do my engagements and not let people down. And they supported me, although they weren't aware how much it carried me through."

༖

On her schedule: "Imagine having to go to a wedding every day of your life—as the bride. Well, that's a bit what it's like."

༖

On adapting to the royal way of life: "I don't think anyone can tell you what's going to happen until you go through the experience yourself. My husband's taught me all I know. I did [find it difficult to adapt], purely because there was so much attention on me when I first arrived on the scene and I wanted to get my act together, so to speak, and I had so many people watching me, the pressure was enormous. But as years go on it gets better. I'm still learning all the time."

༖

"I don't suffer jet lag when I'm coming home east to west. But it really affects me going the other way, west to east. I was fine coming home, but on the way out to Korea I took three sleeping tablets and I still couldn't close my eyes. I was like a zombie when I arrived in Seoul. I was like this [demonstrating her clenched fists and a robotic stare to journalist Arthur Edwards]."

☙

In February 1987, on a royal tour in Vancouver, she collapsed. "I was simply exhausted. It was boiling hot. We hadn't eaten all day because it was a buffet lunch and whenever I put a fork near my mouth, someone else was brought up to me to be introduced."

☙

During a visit to the Turning Point charity for alcoholics in London, she remarked: "I don't drink at all, but I understand the pressures. I am constantly offered drinks at parties and social functions, and I know how difficult it is to resist. Contrary to some reports in sensational newspapers, I can assure you that I have not been drinking and I am not about to become an alcoholic. Everything is geared toward drinking. Whenever I switch on the television soap operas, they seem to center around pub life. In *EastEnders* [a British soap opera], the whole theme is drink and pubs. When I go out for a social thing, I don't drink, and people find that peculiar."

❧

"I have had to learn to rise above criticism. But the irony is that it's been useful in giving me a strength which I did not think I had. That's not to say criticism hasn't hurt me."

❧

One fellow, spotting Diana at lunch, asked if she'd ever been told she looked awfully like the Princess of Wales. "Oh, I know, it's such a bore—we get mistaken for each other all the time."

❧

In the considerable wake of newspaper reports about "the tormented mind of a princess" and allegations about her bulimia, Diana put the matter to rest in a speech to charity workers. "Ladies and gentlemen, you are very lucky to have your patron here today. I am supposed to have my head down

the loo for most of the day.... I am supposed to
be dragged off the minute I leave here by men in
white coats. If it is all right with you, I thought
I would postpone my nervous breakdown to a
more appropriate moment."

❧

Reflecting, in 1995: "[Charles and I] were a very
good team in public; albeit what was going on in
private, we were a good team."

❧

"Being a princess is not all it's cracked up to be."

❧

On the millions of women who dreamed of changing places with her: "They don't know how lucky
they are."

❧

She told journalist and friend Arthur Edwards:
"From now on, it's a strictly hands-on approach. I
want to become more involved with the Red

Cross, for example. No more glitz. Arthur, you don't know how much I hate the glitz. I hate all those premieres, but I have to do some."

※

In November 1993, addressing a mental-health conference in London, Diana seemed to be describing her own emotional state: "There seems to be a growing feeling of . . . emptiness in people's lives. Deep within us all is a need to care and be cared for . . . yet many people, in their attempt to build a life . . . lose touch with their own sense of belonging and of being a part of something greater than themselves."

※

Explaining her semiretirement in December 1993: "I wanted to give one hundred and ten percent to my work, and I could only give fifty. I was constantly tired, exhausted, because the pressure was just, it was so cruel. So I thought the only way to do it was to stand up and make a speech and extract myself before I started disappointing and not carrying out my work. It was my decision to make that speech because I owed it to the public to say that, you know, 'Thank you. I'm disappearing for a bit, but I'll come back.' "

✿

After the semiretirement speech: "I did a lot of work, well, underground, without any media attention, so I never really stopped doing it. I just didn't do every day out and about, I just couldn't do it. You know, the campaign at that point was being successful, but it did surprise the people who were causing the grief—it did surprise them when I took myself out of the game."

✿

Pointing to an outsized medal on her jacket, she told a group of photographers in a Klosters café: "I have awarded it to myself for services to my country, because no one else will."

✿

In 1994, she said to royal reporter James Whitaker, "Would you come to my funeral were I to die? Why would you want to?"

❧

On Patrick Demarchelier's famous informal photographic portraits of her for *Vogue*: "Every photo of me is taken because I am the Princess of Wales, not because I am Diana. I wanted some pictures of the real me, photographed naturally, and not because I am married to Prince Charles. I like what [Patrick] did. I hope everyone else does."

❧

She told *Majesty* magazine editor-in-chief Ingrid Seward: "No one understands what it is like to be me. Not my friends, not anyone."

❧

By 1996, Diana had this to say about the "Queen of Hearts" moniker given to her by the press, in a sense trivializing her good works: "It's my biggest regret. It is embarrassing and keeps coming back to haunt me."

❧

After a particularly exhausting day in Chicago in 1996, an organizer asked Diana how she did it all. She replied, "I am so tired right now I could put my head down on the table and fall asleep." And then she pulled herself up and said, "Commitment and duty."

❦

Diana once told a woman with speech and hearing difficulties: "It's probably just as well you can't hear me very well."

❦

In Sydney she quoted a poem by the Australian Adam Lindsay Gordon: " 'Life is mostly froth and bubble, / Two things stand like stone / Kindness in another's trouble, / Courage in your own.' "

Good Works

"I see myself as a princess for the world, not the Princess of Wales."

✣

"I pay a great deal of attention to people, and I remember them," she told the French newspaper *Le Monde* in her final interview. "Every meeting, every visit is special."

✣

"Being constantly in the public eye gives me a special responsibility, particularly that of using the impact of photographs to transmit a message, to sensitize the world to an important cause, to defend certain values."

✣

"If I must define my role, I'd rather use the word 'messenger.'"

❧

"Anywhere I see suffering, that is where I want to be, doing what I can."

❧

"Nobody can dictate my conduct. I work on instinct. It's my best advisor."

❧

"If I'm going to talk on behalf of any cause, I want to go and see the problem for myself and learn about it."

❧

Diana was caught in a downpour at a charity function in 1991. "I'm like a drowned rat. It's a good job I'm going to a blind home next."

❧

"Nothing would upset me more than just being a name on top of a piece of paper. I think it is important that you should show you are interested and not just breezing in and out."

✻

"There are two basic agents when defining us as human beings—a sharpness of mind and a kindness of heart."

✻

"I am deeply embarrassed when people put me on a pedestal. It is just ridiculous. But... I must do what I can for those poor children."

✻

"The enemy was my husband's [publicity] department, because I always got more publicity, my work ... was discussed much more than him. And, you know, from that point of view I understand it. But I was doing good things, and I wanted to do good things. I was never going to hurt anyone, I was never going to let anyone down."

✻

Speaking at a Relate (a guidance-counseling service) Family of the Year luncheon: "Sadly, many marriages' reality fails to live up to expectations.

We should remember that the Family of the Year Award celebrates the victory of simple values over the complex difficulties confronted by so many marriages."

❧

After the IRA bombed a shopping center in a British village in 1993, killing two children, Diana telephoned the mothers to extend her sympathy. "I'm sorry, I wanted to give you all a big hug, but I'm not allowed to come. My father-in-law is coming instead."

❧

Accepting the Humanitarian of the Year Award in New York in December 1995, she said: "Everyone needs to be valued. Everyone has the potential to give something back if only they had the chance."

❧

Diana told *Le Monde* during her final interview: "Over the years, I had to learn to ignore criticism. But the irony is that it gave me strength that I was far from thinking I had. That doesn't mean it didn't hurt me. To the contrary. But that gave me the strength I needed to continue along the path I had chosen."

☙

Going through photographs of her tours with *Le Monde* journalist Annick Cojean during the final interview, she paused at one picture. "That little boy died," she said, staring fixedly at a photograph taken in 1996 in Pakistan. "I had a foreboding before taking him in my arms. I remember his face, his pain, his voice. . . . This photo is very special to me. . . . If I have to pick one out, without any hesitation, it's this one."

☙

Discussing photographs of herself among the suffering: "It's really a private moment in a public event—a private emotion that a photo turns into public behavior. It's a curious coming together of things. Still, if I had the choice, it's in that kind of surrounding, where I feel perfectly in harmony, that I prefer to be photographed."

※

Diana explained to *Le Monde:* "Yes, I do touch. I believe that everyone needs that, whatever their age. When you put your hand on a friendly face, you make contact right away; you communicate warmth, show that you're close by. It's a gesture that comes to me naturally from the heart. It's not premeditated."

※

Charity director Patricia Ferrall explained to Diana that there was a revolution taking place in the treatment of cerebral palsy patients. Diana rejoined: "Well, you've got the right person, then. I'm the ultimate rebel."

※

"When I go home and turn off my light at night, I know I did my best."

On helping those rejected by society

"Nothing gives me greater happiness than trying to help the weakest in this society. It's a goal and, from now on, an essential part of my life. It's a sort of destiny. I will run to anyone who calls to me in distress, wherever it is."

❧

"I was very confused by which area I should go into. Then I found myself being more and more involved with people who were rejected by society—with, I'd say, drug addicts, alcoholism, battered this, battered that—and I found an affinity there. And I respected very much the honesty I found on that level with people I met, because in hospices, for instance, when people are dying they're much more open and more vulnerable, and much more real than other people. And I appreciated that. . . . No one sat me down with a piece of paper and said: 'This is what is expected of you.' But there again, I'm lucky enough in the fact that I have found my role, and I'm very conscious of it, and I love being with people."

🌺

"I think the biggest disease this world suffers from in this day and age is a disease of people feeling unloved. And I know that I can give love. For a minute, for half an hour, for a day or a month, but I can give and I'm very happy to do that, and I want to do that. It's always been my concern to touch people with leprosy, trying to show in a simple action that they are not reviled, nor are we repulsed."

🌺

"I feel close to people whoever they are—that's why I disturb certain circles. I am much closer to people at the bottom than at the top. I have a real relationship with the most humble people."

🌺

She once told *Vanity Fair*: "Nothing gives me more pleasure now than being able to love and help those in our society who are vulnerable. If I can contribute a little something, then I am more than content."

✻

After visiting a poor family's hut in Nepal, Diana declared: "I will never complain again."

✻

In her final interview for *Le Monde*, Diana mused: "I feel close to people, whoever they are. We're immediately at the same level on the same wavelength. That's why I upset certain circles. It's because I'm much closer to the people at the bottom than the people at the top, and the latter won't forgive me for it. . . . My father always taught me to treat everyone as an equal. I've always done so, and I'm sure that Harry and William will follow in my footsteps."

On comforting the sick and dying

On her late-night visits to the sick and dying in hospitals to comfort them: "It is something I love doing."

✻

"I remember when I used to sit on hospital beds and hold people's hands, people used to be sort of shocked because they'd never seen this before. To me it was quite normal."

✻

"I want to walk into a room, be it a hospice for the dying or a hospital for sick children, and feel that I am needed. I want to do, not just to be."

✻

Comforting angina sufferer Francis Powell when he collapsed in front of her in 1991, she said, "Don't worry, an ambulance is on its way. You're going to be all right now. What a thing to happen—you've given us all quite a fright."

✻

In 1993, she reached out to touch lepers in Nepal "to show that they are not reviled."

✻

When asked whether being with dying people ever drained her, she replied, "No, never. When you discover you can give joy to people like that, there is nothing quite like it. William has begun to understand that, too. And I am hoping it will grow in him."

❧

"I could [visit the sick and dying, refugees, battered women, and homeless shelters] full-time if I could. I don't find it at all exhausting."

❧

Speaking in Chicago about cancer in 1996: "The dreaded C word—it seems to strike from nowhere, destroying lives almost at will, leaving devastation in its wake. But the advances that have been made are quite staggering. It may not always be possible to provide the complete solution to a patient's predicament but does that mean we should give up? Sometimes we may only be able to provide support and counsel. Does that mean we have failed? I think not."

❦

When reminded by her stepmother, Raine, of how hurt her father was by his first wife's desertion, she said, "Pain—Raine, that's one word you don't even know how to relate to. In my role I see people suffer like you'll never see and you call that pain. You've got a lot to learn."

❦

"I so admire you," Diana told Louise Woolcock, a twenty-one-year-old woman dying of cancer. "How angry are you?"

❦

While noting that staggering advances have been made in the fight against cancer, "our work is not yet finished," she said. "I would suggest that now might be a good time to consider another C word which may threaten us. It is the word 'complacency,' and that is why this symposium is of such importance."

❦

In a 1990 address to the International Congress for the Family in Brighton, she said, "There are certain common ingredients essential for families of all sizes and types. There must of course be love, but love is—in its most practical form—commitment to each other, sharing together, self-discipline, and some self-sacrifice. I doubt whether there is any standard formula for a successful family. The family is after all the most human and perfect institution. Instead I could only point to those mothers and fathers and children—in lonely isolation or in conformity—who simply do their best to have what they have. Remember that the very idea of a human family has many definitions and perhaps only those who depend on it most—the young, the old, the sick, and the dying—can really pretend to know its meaning."

꙼

After attending two-and-a-half hours of lifesaving open-heart surgery on a seven-year-old boy in 1996: "I gather information much more from visual contact than from reading books, so when I stand and speak about the various subjects I find

it more beneficial to have actually seen it myself."
She also said, of the surgery, "It is literally seeing
life on a knife-edge. It motivates me and brings
me into my life. I'm a great lover of children. The
fact that a little person can have a second opportunity from my country, I'm very proud to be involved."

❧

At Royal Brompton Hospital in London in early
1996: "I make the trips at least three times a week,
and spend up to four hours at a time with patients
holding their hands and talking to them. Some of
them will live and some will die, but they all need
to be loved while they are here. I try to be there
for them. I really love helping. I seem to draw
strength from them."

On helping the mentally ill

Opening the Ninth Congress of the European
Child and Adolescent Psychiatry, in London: "I do
not believe that emotions are necessarily nuisances

which need to be suppressed or concealed. Sadness is one emotion which often makes observers feel more uncomfortable than those who are sad. As far as I know, crying has yet to kill someone. I am not advocating a general wailing or gnashing of teeth or sackcloth and ashes. But emotional outbursts might be less dramatic or violent if a little steam was to be occasionally vented harmlessly."

❧

On a visit to a hospice for the mentally ill: "After I had been round the first ward, I remember it so vividly, I was struck by the calmness of the patients in their beds, confronting their illness. They were so brave about it and made me feel so humble."

On the deaf community

From her foreword to *The Dictionary of British Sign Language/English:* "As patron of the British Deaf Association, I am delighted to welcome the publication of this unique bilingual *Dictionary of British Sign Language/English*. British Sign Language (BSL) is the fourth most commonly used of Britain's indigenous languages after English, Welsh, and Scottish Gaelic, and is estimated to be the first or preferred language of over 50,000 people in this country. As a consequence of my involvement with deaf people, I have become aware of the richness of BSL as a distinct and independent language. I know this Dictionary will be seen as a welcome and important bridge-building enterprise."

❧

On deaf people and learning British Sign Language: "Well, I'm trying, but I think it's important to show that you're interested and you're not just breezing in and out, having seen [deaf people] for a morning. I've got all my senses and they haven't, and I'm learning how they adapt, or if they've been deaf and dumb since birth, how they cope, and how they deal with the outside world that doesn't always want to know about them."

On the elderly

In 1985, Diana made these remarks at the opening of a Northampton day-care extension to the care home named for her grandmother: "Who would have believed that it was nine years ago that I first came to watch Queen Elizabeth open this nursing home? I must admit that I am more nervous today, as it is the first time that my father and I have shared the same platform. For us, it is a very special family occasion, and I know we all wish my grandmother could be here today to see this fine new building. The extension will enable many more patients living in the community to be given the care they need when they aren't able to cope at home."

※

At the launch of Help the Aged's jubilee celebration: "We have a duty to ensure that the elderly are felt to be valued and important members of our society."

On drug addiction

In 1986, Diana opened the Northeast Council on Addiction in Newcastle. "There are an increasing number of families in this country which have some first-hand knowledge or experience of the despair, misery, and sheer waste of life that the problem of drug addiction causes. We have a battle on our hands. It has to be waged on two major fronts: prevention and cure. As far as prevention is concerned, parents and teachers are in the front line. As a parent myself, I'm only too aware of the responsibility this implies in terms of the kind of upbringing best suited to encourage the child to say no. From the point-of-view of 'cure,' it is vitally important to have adequate facilities available, such as those which allow ex-addicts to run homes or treatment centers for people who have made the decision to try and abandon drugs."

❧

Speaking at the Thirty-sixth International Conference on Alcohol and Drug Abuse in Glasgow, in August 1992: "Addiction removes almost any semblance of social behavior in people who might previously have seemed pleasant. This is termed untrue by some who say that alcohol and alcoholics have contributed inestimably to mankind. Undoubtedly contributions have been made to the world by people who are alcoholics. But I doubt it was the alcohol. Sadly people still regard this as moral weakness. A number of these self-appointed moralists even chose to make such judgments from behind a cloud of cigarette smoke. Presumably they regard cigarette smoking as normal, morally neutral, and nonaddictive. Addiction is a fast-growing malignancy which destroys almost everything in its path. Even those who make money out of it—not just the pushers and dealers—are destroying the society in which they may wish to appear affluent. There is little point in being a gold-plated tin in a dustbin."

※

"For decades, tranquilizers, sleeping pills, and antidepressants have been given to generations of women—three times as many as to men. These 'mother's little helpers' have left a legacy of millions of women doomed to a life of dependence from which there is still very little help to escape."

In a 1993 speech to the Institute for Drug Dependence in New York, Diana said, "Hugging has no harmful side effects. If we all play our part, the result will be tremendous. There are potential huggers in every household."

On AIDS

In April 1987, Diana took off her gloves and held hands with AIDS patient Shane Snape at Britain's first AIDS ward at Middlesex Hospital. She said to Shane, "It must be really difficult for you."

From a speech on AIDS: "HIV does not make people dangerous to know. So you can shake their hands and give them a hug. Heaven knows, they need it. . . . We cannot afford to think of HIV and AIDS as someone else's problem and put it to the back of our minds. If we do, we risk turning what is, in the end, just another life-threatening illness into a plague which will create fear and suspicion in place of goodwill and humanity amongst far more people than will ever feel the effects of the disease."

⁂

After holding a dying black baby with AIDS in a Harlem hospital in 1989: "I felt so sad when I think about how I held that little boy in my arms. It was so moving. Maybe it's because I'm a woman traveling alone. It never feels so bad when my husband is with me."

⁂

At an AIDS conference in 1991: "Don't be so smug. It could be you next."

⁂

Diana's friend, art dealer Adrian Ward Jackson, died of AIDS complications in August 1991, just minutes before she arrived at the hospital. She said: "If more people are now aware of what a dreadful disease AIDS is, then his death will not be in vain. It is an experience I shall never forget."

※

In Cape Town, March 1997: "If I can help in any way [with AIDS prevention in South Africa], then I will do it."

On the homeless

"If an Englishman's home is his castle, then what happens to that young Englishman when he has no home? And if that Englishman is young—perhaps midteens, early twenties—what greater risks will confront him? Neither are the homeless made up of twenty- and thirty-year-olds who've had their chance at life and failed miserably. The age of homeless youngsters is coming down. Children as young as eleven called on Centrepoint [shelter] this year. Some had been running from physical and emotional violence, some from sexual abuse."

※

With her children at her side, she said this to a homeless man in a shelter: "Tonight I am not a princess; my sons are not the two princes. I'm Diana, this is William, and this is Harry. You never look up, you never look down, you look straight ahead."

☙

From her December 1995 speech at her favorite homeless charity: "It is truly tragic to see the total waste of so many young lives, of so much potential. Everyone needs to be valued. Everyone has the potential to give something back, if only they had the chance."

On scaling back

In 1993, in a very emotional address, Diana announced to the National Head Injury Association in London that she would scale back her public duties at the end of that year. "For the past year, I have continued as before; however life and circumstances alter and I hope you will forgive me if I use this opportunity to share with you my plans for the future which now indeed have changed. When I started my public life twelve years ago, I understood the media might be interested in what I did. I realized then their attention would inevitably focus on both our private and public lives. But I was not aware of how overwhelming that attention would become nor the extent to which it would affect both my public duties and my personal life in a manner that's been hard to bear. At the end of this year, when I've completed my diary of official engagements, I will be reducing the extent of the public life I've led so far. Obviously I attach great importance to my charity work and I intend to focus on a smaller range of areas in the future. Over the next few months, I will be seeking a more suitable way of combining a meaningful public role with hopefully a more private life. My first priority will continue to be our children, William and Harry, who deserve as much love and care and attention as I am able to give, as well as an appreciation of the tradition into which they were born. I would like to add that this decision has been reached with the full understanding of the Queen and the Duke of Edinburgh, who have always shown me kindness and support. I hope you can find it in your hearts to understand and to give me the time and space that has been lacking in recent years. I couldn't stand here today and make this sort of statement without acknowledging the heartfelt support I've been given by the public in general."

In a letter written to charities at the time of this decree, she stated: "It has been a great privilege for me to serve as your patron, and it has always been my wish that I should do so wholeheartedly and to the best of my ability. Therefore it is with great sadness that I write to you in order to explain matters which have now become apparent.

"As you know, my personal circumstances, in particular my marriage to the Prince of Wales, have been the subject of detailed conjecture in recent months, and this will soon be formalized in the normal legal manner.

"Although I am embarking on the future with hope, I also do so with some trepidation since there are a number of matters which I shall need to resolve. It is for this reason that I am writing in order to resign my current role as patron with you. As I seek to reorganize my life, it will not be possible for me to provide you with the level of commitment that I feel you deserve. I feel that someone else in the royal family may now be better suited to support your tremendous endeavors. I will always retain a keen interest in everything that you do and trust that we shall have reason for our paths to cross in the not-too-distant future."

On Bosnia

In 1996: "I feel very strongly that I should go to Bosnia, but absolute hell would break out if I did. The Foreign Office would get at me."

❧

"Poverty I have seen in many places, but not war damage of this kind."

On land mines and their victims

At the outset of her land-mine tour in Angola, Diana told the press: "It is an enormous privilege for me to be invited here to Angola in order to assist the Red Cross in its campaign to ban, once and for all, antipersonnel land mines. There couldn't be a more appropriate place to begin this campaign than in Angola."

❧

In a BBC documentary filmed during a visit with mine victims in Angola, Diana proclaimed: "I am not a political figure, nor do I want to be one. But I come with my heart, and I want to bring awareness to people in distress, whether it's in Angola or any other part of the world. The fact is, I'm a humanitarian figure. I always have been, and I will always be."

❧

On the Angolan children wounded by land mines: "I looked into their eyes and saw it all."

❧

"People always say that the eyes mirror the soul. During the last few days [in Angola] I've seen a lot of anguish and a lot of hope in the eyes of people I've met."

❧

In a speech during her antiland-mine campaign, she said: "Having seen for myself the devastation that antipersonnel land mines cause, I am committed to supporting, in whatever way I can, the international campaign to outlaw these dreadful weapons. Achieving a global ban is one step because mines are being laid at the rate of two million a year, but removed at only 100,000 per year. But helping mine victims is equally important."

❧

Jerry White, a cofounder of the Landmine Survivors Network who lost his legs to a mine, explained to Diana before they were to fly from London to Sarajevo in a six-seater Lear Jet that in any airplane it's more comfortable for amputees to remove their prostheses. "Oh, my God, you're taking off your legs?" she blurted out. White remembers, however, that "she went with the program."

Joking with a one-armed man: "I'll bet you have fun chasing the soap round the bath!"

"The mine is a stealthy killer. Long after conflict has ended, its innocent victims die or are wounded singly, in countries of which we hear little. Their lonely fate is never reported. The world, with its other many preoccupations, remains largely unmoved. . . ."

"When you look at the mangled bodies of children caught by these mines, you marvel at their survival."

"Much ingenuity has gone into making some of these mines. Many are designed to trap an unwary de-miner. Whenever such tricky mines appear, the de-miner will call in one of the supervising teams who will then take over. That is what keeps their lives perpetually at risk."

※

"There are said to be around one hundred and ten million mines lurking somewhere in the world, and over a third of them are to be found in Africa! Angola is probably more heavily mined than anywhere else because the war went on for such a long time."

※

"Even if the world decided tomorrow to ban these weapons, this terrible legacy of mines already in earth would continue to plague the poor nations of the globe."

※

"The more expeditiously we can end this plague on earth caused by the land mine, the more readily can we set about the constructive task to which so many give their hand in the cause of humanity."

"I was briefed but it did not prepare me for the reality. I have never seen scenes like this before. It is very humbling. Being a mother of two boys, one wants to go out and help these children in particular where little people have lost their legs. Part of their future has been taken away. It's had a tremendous impact on me. But when you're traumatized to the extent these people have, the only thing you can hang on to is your dignity. No one can take that away."

"It's horrific. . . . Someone's got to do something. There was a little girl with her intestines blown out and she was very, very poorly. Just looking at her and thinking what was going on inside her head was very disturbing. But she's just one statistic."

❧

"My lasting impression is of the hope that's generated in my country. They have so many problems. I've had both ends of the spectrum—some of it official but most of it informal. You have to have one with the other, but I've always wanted to do visits like this.

❧

"The Red Cross originally suggested me going to other countries but it was not appropriate. It was suggested that we should go to Angola, which was sensible as it is the country most affected by land mines. The number of amputees is quite shocking."

❧

Former land-mine clearer Chris Moon was maimed by a mine, but he carries on in any way he can—usually by performing feats of physical endurance—to draw attention to the cause of banning land mines. Diana said of him: "He really symbolizes what selfless bravery is."

At a Washington gala dinner to aid the American Red Cross, in June 1997, Diana said, "I do so welcome this opportunity to share with you all some experiences of the waste of life, limb, and land which antipersonnel land mines are causing amongst some of the poorest people on earth. Permit me not to tell you exactly what I saw. What is so cruel about these wounds is they are almost invariably suffered where medical resources are scarce. A chronic shortage of medicine, of pain killers, even of anaesthetics. Surgeons engaged in amputating limbs without the facilities we would expect to see here. The evil that men do lives after them. . . ."

In a BBC documentary about land mines in Angola, Diana said, "Before I came to Angola, I knew the facts, but the reality was a shock. Here people are living with the knowledge that it is only a matter of time before someone else is maimed or killed. It was moving and encouraging to see the confidence shown by those learning to walk again."

❧

Blowing up a mine by remote control, she said, "One down, ten million to go."

❧

When she learned that her efforts in Angola had been turned into a political football back in England, she said, "I think I'm going to burst into tears now."

❧

A government minister referred to Diana as a "loose cannon," forcing her to respond that she was "just trying to help" land-mine victims. "I am only trying to highlight a problem that's going on around the world. That's all."

❧

"I can't tell you how much the land-mines movement means to me. But when I did that, you criticized me. I'm accused of being political, but I'm not; I just want to help people. I saw the [reaction among London politicos] as merely a distraction, which meant things went off the rails for five minutes and went back on again. It's not helpful—things like that—but it does happen when a campaign is entwined with a political issue. I understand that."

※

To Richard Kay, on politicians accusing her of meddling in things she didn't understand—namely, the issue of land mines: "What *is* there to understand when people are having their legs blown off?"

※

"[The British Labour party's] position on the subject [of land mines] was always clear. It's going to do tremendous work. Its predecessor was so hopeless. I hope we manage to persuade the United States to sign the treaty ban in Ottawa this December."

※

"The [Tory] polemics [over Diana's Angola mine-field journey] ruined a day's work, but it multiplied the press coverage."

On the plight of women

Mothers "retreat into their own private hell behind closed doors, terrified to go out of their homes into what, to them, has become a frightening world."

❦

"Isn't it normal not to be able to cope all the time? Isn't it normal for women as well as men to feel frustrated with life? Isn't it normal to feel angry and want to change a situation that is hurting?"

❦

"If we, as a society, continue to disable women by encouraging them to believe they should only do things that are thought to benefit their family, even if these women are 'damaged' in the process; if they feel they never have the right to do anything that is just for themselves; if they feel they must sacrifice everything for their loved ones, even at the cost of their own health, their inner strength, and their own self-worth, they will live only in the shadow of others, and their mental health will surely suffer."

Children

"Diana touched the child in each and every one of us." (Ingrid Seward, editor in chief, *Majesty* magazine)

❦

"It's amazing how much happiness a small child brings to people."

❦

In October 1987, Diana told an inquiring play group in Hillington, West London: "Two children is quite enough at the moment. I don't think I'd like to have three boys, although deep down I would love a girl."

❦

"Wouldn't it be lovely to have a daughter who wanted to be with you all the time?"

❧

"Contrary to what you may have heard, I'd like lots and lots more children. I'd love a little girl but I'm wondering whether the world is ready for another me."

❧

At a party early in 1988, she told a friend who has two daughters: "If I have another son and you have another daughter, we'll swap."

❧

On the fact that both of her pregnancies were difficult: "If men had babies, they would only have one each."

❧

"I just can't resist some young children. They stand before me, some with their arms stretched out. I just want to pick them up in my arms, so I do."

❧

In Australia, Diana met a woman with a fractious baby who told her that she wished she had a nanny to take care of her child. Diana said, "I would swap with you anytime. I wish I didn't have to leave William with a nanny. I would rather do what you are doing."

❧

"To encourage and guide, to nourish and nurture, and to listen with love to their needs in ways which clearly show our children that we value them. They in their turn will then learn how to value themselves."

❧

"Some psychologists believe that problems start in the womb. Morning sickness can affect both mother and child. Cigarettes and alcohol can restrict the child's growth potential; so can anguish or violence around the mother. The outside world they are meant to be joining soon seems less attractive than the warmth of the womb. Often the conflict between parents can distract either parent from meeting the needs of the children, or worse still, the children become pawns in their parents' struggle. Parents sometimes desert families, leaving their children bewildered and bereft with no explanation. Like crying, cuddles or hugs don't hurt. It is cheap, environmentally friendly, and needs minimal instruction. It is a simple and highly effective way of sharing concern or showing approval."

❧

She told an eleven-year-old, who'd greeted her with "Good morning, Princess Diana," "Oh, no, I do not want you to call me Princess. Just call me Diana."

❧

When a little girl who had failed to get close enough to Diana to hand her a bouquet of flowers burst out sobbing, Diana bent down to take the flowers from her, reassuring her: "Agony over."

❧

"I made the grave mistake once of saying to a child I was thick as a plank, in order to ease the child's nervousness, which it did. But that headline went all round the world, and I rather regret saying it."

※

Diana wrote the young daughter of *Majesty* magazine's editor: "I hope for your birthday you managed to get those grown-ups to give you the doll's house and the cardigan and the pony hairbrush. Don't believe their excuses."

※

"I think of parents who this very night are standing around a hospital bed, not knowing if their children will wake in the morning."

※

During a visit to the Childline Charity Headquarters in London, she wondered aloud: "How do your counselors manage to listen to this every day and not take it home with them? How can children experience that kind of harm and grow up into loving parents?"

✿

In 1988, Diana addressed the Annual Conference of Dr. Barnardo's, a charity devoted to caring for orphaned and disabled children: "I have seen . . . efforts made to help families remain together and in the work undertaken to provide foster homes or personal residential care for those young people unable to live with their own families. Recently, I visited three projects which, in quite separate ways, were examples of family life bringing new hope, help, and security to children and young people in very varied circumstances.

"In Liverpool, for instance, it was the family of a profoundly handicapped teenager. In this case, the demands made on her parents were so great that when young, her parents had no option but to place her in a long-stay hospital. After many years in the hospital, she went to live at [a care home], where the experience of having personal, committed care, linked with a carefully worked-out learning program, has enabled her to make enormous progress. Now this young woman spends each weekend with her parents, and the weekdays

with Barnardo's. A fine example of a family re-
united.

"I fully realized that for many people, family
life is not always a happy experience. They may
have been thrown out of their homes, or circumstances may have forced them to leave. Some are
homeless. Others are at risk of drug addiction or
prostitution. It's even more of a challenge if such
young adults are also parents. In Leeds I met one
young woman with her five-month-old baby who,
after several years in care, is now being helped by
Barnardo's to establish a home with her boyfriend
and to provide some real security for her child.

"As a mother of two small boys I think we may
have to find a securer way of helping our children—to nurture and prepare them to face life as
stable and confident adults. The pressures and demands on all of us are enormous. I do realize that
the view of what constitutes a family life is
broader today than it was a century ago. Today
few children lose parents through early death, but
many do experience that loss through divorce, and
increasingly more complicated families result
from separation and remarriage. A statistic which

brings this home is that one in eight children live in single-parent families. These children's experience of family life may be different, but I do not believe that it need be any less satisfying or effective. When the good doctor [Barnardo] started his work at the end of the last century, he was concerned with orphans. Today, over a century later, the organization which carries his name, while still deeply involved in the care of children, is now working with children and their families. I have been asked today to reveal to you all Barnardo's new identity. I believe and hope you will agree with me that it captures many of the elements which are important in family life: commitment, togetherness, and building the way ahead to the future."

❦

On her work with Barnado's: "I'm going out there to meet those children and I'm learning all the time. I'm trying desperately to understand how they cope."

❦

"It's customary at this year of year to focus attention on those less fortunate than ourselves. But homelessness is an experience which isn't confined to the festive season. It is a daily problem."

❦

"I'm appalled at the dangers young people face on the streets and how vulnerable they are to exploitation. Sixteen- and seventeen-year-olds who resort to begging, or worse, prostitution, to get money in order to eat. Young people whose physical and mental health has been severely damaged by life on the streets. Young people who take drugs to provide some escape from the hardship they face. Young people who've been attacked and abused on the streets and face the indifferent stares of passersby who have no idea how brave they are or how much they've suffered."

❦

In Angola she met many children who had been maimed by land mines. "When you see little children like that in that situation it just brings it all to the surface. It makes me very sad, what I have seen. It's very traumatic as a mother to witness this."

※

"If we can do a proper job of giving our children the affection which nature demands, I believe it will help enormously. Hugging has no harmful side effects."

The Media

About *The Washington Post* matriarch Katharine Graham, whom former *New Yorker* editor Tina Brown described as "the kind of social protector that Diana always lacked," Diana said simply, "I love her. I really do."

⚜

When she learned that journalist Anthony Holden was working on a book called *The Tarnished Crown*, she told his wife: "Perhaps it should be called 'The Tarnished Tiara'?"

⚜

Before the wedding, the media hunger was already beyond ravenous. One reporter told her she seemed to be bearing up quite well. "It must be quite a strain with all of us after you," he said. "Well, it is naturally," she replied. "You seem to be doing very well," he continued. "Well, I'm still around."

※

"I was very daunted [by all the attention] because as far as I was concerned I was a fat, chubby, twenty-year-old, twenty-one-year-old, and I couldn't understand the level of interest."

※

One of the first photographs of Diana proved to be one of the most infamous. She stood in a garden with two of her kindergarten students, with the sun behind her, revealing her bare legs through her cotton skirt. Neither she nor the photographers were aware of this. "I was so nervous about the whole thing. I never thought I'd be standing with the light behind me. I don't want to be remembered for not having a petticoat."

※

She told *Majesty* editor-in-chief Ingrid Seward: "It makes me feel insecure, and it is difficult going out and meeting people when I imagine what they might have read about me that morning."

❦

On the press: "I love working with children, and I have learned to be very patient with them."

❦

"I just can't win. They either accuse me of spending too much on clothes or of wearing the same outfit all the time. I wish everyone would stop talking about my clothes."

❦

"The most daunting aspect [of my public life] was the media attention, because my husband and I, we were told when we got engaged that the media would go quietly, and it didn't; and then when we were married they said it would go quietly, and it didn't; and then it started to focus very much on me, and I seemed to be on the front of a newspaper every single day, which is an isolating experience, and the higher the media put you, place you, the bigger is the drop. And I was very aware of that."

🌺

"Here was a situation which hadn't ever happened before in history, in the sense that the media were everywhere, and here was a fairy story that everybody wanted to work. And so it was, it was isolating, but it was also a situation where you couldn't indulge in feeling sorry for yourself: You had to either sink or swim. And you had to learn that very fast."

🌺

"It was difficult to share that load [of media fascination], because I was the one who was always pitched out front, whether it was my clothes, what I said, what my hair was doing, everything— which was a pretty dull subject, actually, and it's been exhausted over the years—when actually what we wanted to be, what we wanted supported was our work, and as a team."

🌺

"It took a long time to understand why people were so interested in me, but I assumed it was because my husband had done a lot of wonderful work leading up to our marriage and our relationship. But then you [start to] see yourself as a good product that sits on a shelf and sells well, and people make a lot of money out of you."

❀

"We struggled a bit with [the media interest], it was very difficult; and then my husband decided that we do separate engagements, which was a bit sad for me, because I quite liked the company."

❀

She couldn't understand why the press portrayed her as someone who disapproved of country pursuits. "After all, I was brought up in that way. I hunted when I was young. And it is all part of their heritage."

❀

By 1985, Diana had developed a somewhat thicker skin when it came to the press. "You've got to push yourself out and remember that some people, hopefully, don't believe everything they read about you."

❀

To a group of journalists in London: "The only thing you don't know about me is how many fillings I've had."

❀

Journalist and friend Arthur Edwards complained that she'd worn "that boring old dress" at the opera the previous night. She rejoined, "Oh, I suppose you'd like it better if I came naked."

❀

She told journalist Anthony Holden: "I can never enjoy any weekend until I know someone else is on the front page of the *News of the World*."

❀

When Arthur Edwards complained to her that he'd broken a few ribs falling off a ladder while photographing Diana in Lisbon the previous week, she cracked, "Oh, I knew it would be my fault."

❧

She told a group of journalists at a party: "There I was in this leprosy mission in the hills of Nepal and I look across the room, and what do I see? A *Vogue* T-shirt! I thought, Oh, no, not *here*!"

❧

Diana particularly despised the British press. "There is an obsessive interest in me and the children."

❧

Paparazzo Glenn Harvey asked, "What do you want? No pictures at all?" "*Yes*," she replied. "I'm desperate for that."

❧

Teasing Arthur Edwards one day as she was about to board a very steep escalator: "I suppose you want to take a picture right up my legs?"

❧

"I'm not asking to be perfect. I'm far from it. But I'd just like the chance and opportunity to get involved in my various interests that I've chosen without people talking about me being a shopaholic or something."

❧

"Like it or not, I've been quite a provider for the media. And now I'm asking for your help to reduce the suffering caused by drugs."

❧

While skiing in the Alps, she begged the paparazzi to put their cameras away. "As a parent, could I ask you to respect my children's space because I've brought the children out here for a holiday. . . and we'd really appreciate the space."

❧

"I long ago have given up reading the lurid tabloids, who profess to know what is going on in my life. But I am told what they are saying because of the letters I receive from the public. Of course, I take note when unpleasant post arrives, but there's not much I can do, except carry on doing my job in the best way I can."

※

In July 1986, after Prince Andrew's engagement to Fergie was announced, she said to the paparazzi: "You don't need me anymore, do you?"

※

On duty in the Bahamas, Arthur Edwards complained to Diana that he got the same rate no matter where he photographed. She replied, "Oh, pass me the Kleenex."

※

When Charles tried to ban all contact with the media, she told Edwards: "I do enjoy our chats. My husband refuses to have these parties with the press, but I think they are a good idea. After all, you only need to tell people what they want to know."

❦

"There is too much about me in the newspapers. Far too much. It horrifies me, when there's more important things, like what goes on in the hospices, or when there's been a bomb or something."

❦

Responding to allegations that she and Fergie had been swigging too much champagne at a luncheon, Diana said, "Contrary to recent reports in some of our more sensational Sunday newspapers, I have not been drinking. And I am not, I assure you, about to become an alcoholic."

❦

In the affidavit she submitted to obtain a restraining order against a photographer who had bumped her car with his motorcycle during a pursuit, she wrote that she was "too distraught to leave my home."

❦

She shouted at more than one photographer: "You make my life hell."

🌾

A *Vanity Fair* photographer found Diana so engagingly open that he jokingly said he felt he couldn't call her "ma'am." "Then by all means, call me Diana," she said.

🌾

"You're harassing me! Do you know what it is like? Every time I leave my house you follow me. I know where you sit and watch me. I know where you get your information."

🌾

To Glenn Harvey, who was trying to take a picture of her getting into her new Audi: "I'm just a mother taking my children out for the day. Can't you understand that?" (Harvey had said, "We were told to get a picture of your car." Diana retorted, "But you got it last week. I had fifteen of you following me on a daily basis last week.")

More comments for the persistent Harvey

"Do you know what it's like for me? I have to sit in darkness with the curtains drawn all day. I even had GMTV outside my balcony this morning. Why can't you people just go away?"

❀

"I just want to be left alone."

❀

"But you *do* bother me. Why don't you go away?"

❀

By 1994, she had come to the very end of her tether with the invasive and ubiquitous photographers. "Why, why, why?" she shrieked at them.

❀

When photographer Mark Saunders called her "Your Royal Highness," she snapped, "Don't call me that! It's a sign of respect and you have none for me."

"I don't want [fame]. If it doesn't stop I'm going to leave the country. I'll take the product elsewhere."

Her stock response in confronting the paparrazi in the last years was: "Why don't you go and rape someone else?"

"The press is ferocious," she said to *Le Monde* during her final interview. "It pardons nothing. It looks only for mistakes. Every intention is twisted, every gesture criticized. I think things are different abroad. I'm greeted with kindness. I'm accepted as I am, without prejudices, without watching for every faux pas. In Britain it's the other way round. And I think that in my place, any sane person would have left long ago. But I can't. I have my sons to think about."

Fashion

Did she spend a lot of time thinking about clothes? "No. . . . Just first thing in the morning when I decide what I'm going to wear that day."

🌿

On choosing her outfits: "You'd be amazed what one has to worry about, from the obvious things like the wind—because there is always a gale wherever we go and the wind is my enemy, there's no doubt about that."

🌿

To a group of journalists on the clothes she wore: "Clothes are for the job. They've got to be practical. Sometimes I can be a little outrageous, which is nice, but only sometimes."

🌿

"My clothes are not my priority. I enjoy bright colors, and my husband likes to see me look smart, presentable, but fashion isn't my big thing at all."

🌿

She once recalled the clothes she wore during the early days of her public life: "It's like getting dressed to go to a wedding every day, and when you see yourself photographed in black and white, all the little mistakes show."

🌿

Diana's choice to wear a stunning strapless dress the evening she was to meet Princess Grace of Monaco caused a considerable stir. "I don't know why everyone is making such a fuss," she said to Charles's valet. "It's the sort of dress I would have worn anyway."

🌿

"When I wear a backless dress, I find that most people just don't know where to put their hands."

🌿

After a particularly short haircut, journalist Arthur Edwards remarked that if she kept it up she'd end up looking like pop star Sinead O'Connor. Glancing at his bald pate, she quipped, "At least I've got some hair, Arthur."

❦

"I don't mind if [the jewelry I wear] is fake or real, it makes no difference to me."

❦

"[Tiaras] either give me a terrible headache or they fall down over my forehead, pushing my hair into my eyes. I hate wearing them."

❦

On why her hemline is weighted with a bit of lead: "You've got to put your arm up to get some flowers, and you can't have anything too revealing. And you can't have hems too short because when you bend over there are six children looking up your skirt."

❦

On offering her high-heeled shoes to her sister: "Here, try on my tart's trotters."

❧

She told her sister Jane: "I just love to get home and kick off my shoes, take off my smart clothes, and get into jeans and a sweater. Then I really feel like myself, the real me."

The Royal Family

Diana to Queen Elizabeth: "I will never let you down."

⁂

"I didn't have any idea what I let myself in for. One day, I was going to work on a Number Nine bus and the next, I was a princess."

⁂

In 1994, Diana told the *Times* of London editor Peter Stothard: "My husband's father once sent me a long formal letter setting out the duties of the Princess of Wales. There was 'much [more] to it than being popular,' he said. I sent him back a long letter in reply. He sent me a shorter one. And so on until I finally signed off with, 'It's been so nice getting to know you like this.' One day these letters will be found in the archives. So will the memos by which my husband and I communicate too. Can you believe it?"

🌿

"My [maternal] grandmother tried to lacerate me in any way she could. She fed the royal family with hideous comments about my mother, so whenever I mentioned her, the royal family always came down on me like a ton of bricks. Mummy came across very badly because Grandmother did a real hatchet job."

🌿

After lunching with the Queen: "I was sitting there and the corgis came yapping all around me when I suddenly realized they were fascinated by my red tights. I thought, My God, what if they think my legs are steak? I had visions of the whole lot of them tearing into me and devouring my legs. I nearly burst out laughing but managed to suppress it. I wish I hadn't worn those wretched tights though. I couldn't wait to get out of there."

❧

On Fergie: "I really envy Sarah's freedom."

❧

To Fergie: "They think we were crazy to start with, but we didn't get crazy until we married into this family."

❧

In 1986, she and Fergie dressed up as police-women and raided Prince Andrew's stag party. "Did you see what I did the other night? Didn't it cause a stir? You have to have a laugh some-times. The wig was hot and uncomfortable, and my feet were killing me. The shoes were two sizes too small."

❧

"When I go to the Palace for a garden party or a summit meeting, I am a very different person. I conform to what is expected of me so that they can't find fault when I am in their presence."

❦

"Princess Anne has been working terribly hard for the Save the Children Fund and I'm her biggest fan because of what she crams into a day I could never achieve. We've always hit it off and I think she's marvelous."

❦

But Diana and Princess Anne did not get along particularly well. Diana once dismissed her sister-in-law as a female impersonator. "I think she shaves," she said. When a friend pointed out that Anne was the only female competitor at the Montreal Olympics not to have been given a sex test, Diana joked, "Results would've been too embarrassing. She's Philip—in drag." As for Philip: "The man has the warmth of a snow pea."

❦

"I am performing a duty as the Princess of Wales as long as my time is allocated. But I don't see it any longer than fifteen years."

❦

On her relationship with the Queen: "I was a lamb to the slaughter."

❦

"Maybe I was the first person ever to be in this family who ever had a depression or was ever openly tearful. And obviously that was daunting, because if you've never seen it before how do you support it?"

❦

"From the first day I joined that family, nothing could be done naturally anymore."

❦

"I was the separated wife of the Prince of Wales, I was a problem, full stop. Never happened before, what do we do with her?"

❦

"[The royal family] hadn't expected [the speech announcing her semiwithdrawal from public life].

And I'm a great believer that you should always confuse the enemy."

✤

"Once or twice, I've heard people say: 'Diana's out to destroy the monarchy,' which has bewildered me, because why would I want to destroy something that is my children's future?"

✤

"I tried again and again to get [the royals] to hire someone like [political strategist and media dynamo Peter Mandelson] to give them proper advice, but they didn't want to hear it. They kept saying I was manipulative. But what's the alternative? To just sit there and have them make your image for you? Sometimes editors at newspapers would write editorials suggesting things they could do, but instead of paying attention one of the private secretaries would ring up and give the editors a rocket."

✤

Diana sometimes compared the royal family with the Mafia. "The only difference," she told her cousin, "is these muggers wear crowns."

❦

She was amused when several other members of the royal family copied her dresses. "At least I got to wear them first."

❦

When, at lunch, former *New Yorker* editor Tina Brown suggested that Fergie's "antics" don't help the royal cause, Diana replied, "No, and it's a shame for Andrew, because he really is the best of the bunch. I mean, people don't know this, but he works really, really hard for the country. He does so much, and no one pays any attention at all. It's the same with Princess Anne. She works like a dog, and nobody cares. And I keep saying to Prince Charles, 'It's no good complaining that people don't care about your work. Until you straighten your head out and get things clear, people just won't give you a break.'"

Affairs

"There were three of us in this marriage, so it was a bit crowded."

"I remember I asked him once why he spent so much time with Camilla [Parker Bowles], a married woman. He just shrugged his shoulders and said, 'Because she is safe.' At the time I thought the friendship was what he was talking about; that it was safe for them to be friends because she was married and no one would gossip. What I quickly came to realize was that he meant Camilla was safe because he could carry on sleeping with her and no one would suspect a thing, presumably, least of all, me. What really infuriated me was that the next time I saw Camilla, she patted me on the shoulder and told me 'not to worry' about her. I thought about it later and it was obvious Charles had told her I was worried about her. He told that woman everything. I didn't just marry Charles; I married his mistress too. There was nothing that went on in my marriage she didn't know about."

※

After a dinner at Buckingham Palace: "The Queen stressed the importance of making the marriage work. She told me Charles was willing to give it another go. I promised I would do my best. But I insisted he end his friendship with Camilla. I remember the Queen looking at me over her glasses and saying, 'Why are you so concerned about Camilla? All men have certain urges. Camilla is married, she is no threat to you. Try to put her out of your head. You have nothing to concern yourself with there, my dear.'"

※

"I was [aware of Charles's relationship with Camilla], but I wasn't in a position to do anything about it." The evidence? "Oh, a woman's instinct is a very good one. . . . Well, I had, obviously I had knowledge of it . . . from people who minded and cared about our marriage. [But I could tell Charles was being unfaithful] by the change of behavioral pattern in my husband; for all sorts of reasons that a woman's instinct produces; you just know."

❧

"The Camilla thing reared its head the whole way through our engagement, and I was desperately trying to be mature about the situation, but I didn't have the foundations to do it, and I couldn't talk to anyone about it."

❧

Diana often referred to Camilla as "the Rottweiler."

❧

"The Rottweiler is the main reason why I'm going through this hell. I honestly believe if [Camilla] disappeared, I would at least have a chance to try and make Charles love me. But with that woman around, I have no chance. He's not even thinking about me; all he cares about is Camilla."

❦

"What I simply cannot understand is what he sees in [Camilla]. I mean, she's hardly an oil painting. And she is so blunt and rude. What the hell has she got that I haven't?"

❦

On finding the four-poster bed she and Charles had shared was unmade, the sheets crumpled and slept in, the Princess then ran into the spare bedrooms; none was disturbed. "I was hysterical. It was clear the main bed, *our* bed, *my* marital bed, had been slept in by two people. I went downstairs and screamed at him for sleeping with that woman in my bed. He wouldn't answer. I was shouting at him and crying but he wouldn't say anything. I kept asking him why he was bonking her. It was the worst moment ever. I felt like it was all over. I knew for sure he was sleeping with that bitch. I seriously thought about topping myself there and then. I knew there was no chance. I knew he loved her and not me—and always had done."

❦

The media constantly compared her with Camilla. "It's all so meaningless," she said despairingly.

❦

At last, she confronted Camilla: "Why don't you just leave my husband alone?"

❦

Having been accused of making nuisance phone calls to art dealer Oliver Hoare—hanging up if his wife answered, and so on—Diana told the *Daily Mail*'s royal correspondent, Richard Kay, that she had been framed. "What are they trying to do to me? I feel I am being destroyed. There is no truth in it. . . . It is true that I have called Oliver Hoare, but not in the way alleged."

❦

On the Oliver Hoare phone calls: "I was reputed to have made three hundred telephone calls in a very short space of time which, bearing in mind my lifestyle at that time, made me a very busy lady. But that . . . was a huge move to discredit me, and very nearly did me in, the injustice of it, because I did my own homework on that subject, and consequently found out that a young boy had done most of them."

❦

On the notion of making the Hoare annoyance phone calls from public telephones: "You cannot be serious. I don't even know how to use a parking meter, let alone a phone box."

❦

On Oliver Hoare himself: "They are trying to make out I was having an affair with this man or that it was some sort of *Fatal Attraction.* It is simply untrue and so unfair. Do you realize that whoever is trying to destroy me is inevitably damaging the institution of monarchy as well? I know there are those whose wish is apparently to grind my face in it. I knew I could not rely on anyone sticking up for me, but nor could I allow such hurtful things to be said about me in silence any longer."

❦

She once told her lover James Hewitt: "I am surrounded by people but so alone."

❦

Also to James Hewitt: "My God, if you go ahead with this book [about their affair], it's going to kill me."

❦

When Anna Pasternak's book, *Princess in Love,* written with James Hewitt, was published, the only official comment from Diana at the time: "[I am] extremely upset by the book's account of [my] friendship with Mr. Hewitt. It is simply not true that we ever had sex. He wanted to, but I never let it happen. He lives in a fantasy world."

❦

To deflect the Hewitt rumors, at her birthday luncheon she said: "I'm going to celebrate my birthday at home alone with the only man in my life tonight: Prince Harry."

Squidgygate

In 1990, a taped telephone conversation held on New Year's Eve 1989 between Diana and her dashing friend James Gilbey, a one-time second-hand car dealer, was leaked to the press, where it made headlines for what seemed weeks. These excerpts should demonstrate why, in addition to the profusion of exchanged kisses during the conversation.

❧

JAMES: You don't mind it, darling, when I want to talk to you so much?
DIANA: No, I *love* it. Never had it before.
JAMES: Darling, it's so nice being able to help you.
DIANA: You do. You'll never know how much.
JAMES: Oh, I will, darling. I just feel so close to you. I'm wrapping you up, protecting.
DIANA: Yes, please.

❧

DIANA: I don't want to get pregnant.
JAMES: Darling, that's not going to happen. All right?
DIANA: (chuckle) Yeah.
JAMES: Don't think like that. It's not going to happen, darling. You won't get pregnant.

❧

On a luncheon with members of the royal family: "I was very bad at lunch. And I nearly started blubbing. I just felt really sad and empty, and I thought, Bloody hell, after all I've done for this fucking family."

❧

"[There is] always . . . innuendo . . . that I'm going to do something dramatic because I can't stand the confines of this marriage."

❧

"[Charles and I] went out to tea. It's so difficult, so complicated. He makes my life real torture, I've decided."

❈

On the Queen Mother: "His grandmother is always looking at me with a strange look in her eyes. It's not hatred. It's sort of interest and pity mixed in one. I am not quite sure. I don't understand it. Every time I look up, she's looking at me and then looks away and smiles."

❈

"[Fergie] can't [tag on to my coattails]. If you want to be like me, you have to suffer."

❈

"The redhead [Fergie] is being actually quite supportive. . . . I don't know why."

After the release of the tape

"The implications of that [Squidgygate] conversation were that we'd had an adulterous relationship, which was not true."

✻

"I felt very protective about James because he'd been a very good friend to me . . . , and I couldn't bear that his life was going to be messed up because he had the connection with me. And that worried me. I'm very protective about my friends."

✻

Diana said she had no idea how the "Squidgy" tape came to be published in the national press. "But it was done to harm me in a serious manner, and that was the first time I'd experienced what it was like to be outside the net, so to speak, and not be in the family. [The tape was leaked to the press] to make the public change their attitude towards me."

✻

After the "Squidgy" tape incident Diana said, "I ain't going anywhere. I haven't got a single supporter in this family, but they are not going to break me."

She told a friend that "Squidgygate was a catharsis, really."

Christie's Auction

On June 25, 1997, seventy-nine of Diana's dresses and gowns were auctioned at Christie's in New York, raising $3.26 million for AIDS and cancer charities.

❦

"I am extremely happy to have this wonderful opportunity to raise money for charities devoted to the care of cancer and AIDS sufferers both here in the United Kingdom and in America. It goes without saying that I am also delighted that these dresses, which gave me so much pleasure, may be enjoyed by others."

❦

"Clothes are now not as essential to my work as they used to be."

❦

"I am amazed and a little concerned at the enormous prices for my dresses which are being quoted because it may deter people. What I would say is do please have a try. There will, I'm sure, be some dresses which will be reasonable: I hope that whoever does acquire them will enjoy them and get as much pleasure from them as I did myself."

�֍

Gesturing to the stuffed bank of wardrobes she'd worn on tours: "Now you can see my problem for yourself."

✖

"The inspiration for this wonderful sale comes from just one person . . . our son William."

✖

When a director of Christie's implied that one of the gowns looked "a little tired," Diana replied, "Hardly surprising. I wore it at so many banquets, it must be exhausted."

✖

Columnist Cindy Adams asked Diana how the gowns could be in such perfect condition. Didn't she ever spill on herself? "Of course I did," Diana replied. "I've spilled gravy, and I've spilled shrimps down my front. I'm just like everybody else. But the Palace has wonderful cleaners."

☙

"I've kept a few things. But you know that Catherine Walker [gown] with all the bugle beads? People in England don't wear those kinds of clothes anymore."

Miscellaneous

As of June 1987 Diana's list of preferred activities included dancing, tennis, needlepoint, television ("especially soap operas—*Crossroads, EastEnders, Dallas, Dynasty*"), movies ("James Bond, Ken Russell, old black-and-white weepies"), books (romantic novels like those by Danielle Steel are particular favorites), and theater ("I go as often as I can to the theater").

❧

"I dance once a week if I can. It's a combination of tap, jazz, and ballet. I think it's vital to switch for one or two hours every week. It's my absolute passion. I'm a great believer in having music wherever I go. It's just a big treat to go out for a walk with music still coming out with me. I tend to listen to an enormous amount of classical music. All my family, my side of the family, are very music-oriented, and that's where I picked it up. I love it."

✣

"I get so few chances to go dancing and there's nothing I love more."

✣

Her favorite group: Dire Straits. Her favorite singer: Kiri Te Kanawa. As for food: "I prefer fish to meat. I'm an avid cook."

✣

Some of her favorite "upper-class" expressions included "all this fuss," "quite daunting," "absolutely maddening," "very cross," and the famous "pretty amazing."

✣

Her dislikes: "People who talk about horses all the time," smoking ("I have a no smoking sign in my sitting room"), children with sticky hands, noises in the night, Balmoral ("too big, too cold, and too formal"), royal tours ("I find them exhausting, they make me nervous, and I am often unable to eat"), big dogs in the house.

❦

When a young man with AIDS told her she was "more gorgeous than in the papers," she quickly replied, "You should see me in the mornings."

❦

When handing out the Arts Council's Year of Dance Awards in London: "Dance is one of my greatest loves. It is one of the best ways I know of expressing the joy of living. Dance is a universal language with a unique ability to express human ideas and emotions to bring people together."

❦

A hat-fitter was overwhelmed by the size of her head. She replied, "Don't worry, there's really very little inside."

❦

She turned to an army officer when she was about to drive a tank and said, "I hope it's well insured."

❧

After seeing the London premiere of the movie *Wall Street,* which featured some scenes of steamy sex, she said, "It was much too grown-up for me. I didn't really understand any of it."

❧

When friends Richard and Joan Branson got married after fourteen years and two children, Diana sent a note: "A million congratulations. I am so glad you took the time to think about it."

❧

Diana, an avid swimmer, was asked how she got the chlorine smell out of her hair. "Haven't you heard of shampoo?" she teased.

❧

To inquiring Japanese journalists, she explained, "I don't know why there are all these stories saying I am too thin. I am eating a lot."

❧

Diana openly enjoyed the company of gay men. She enjoyed camping it up herself. "You'd better call me Diana, because I'm a princess and everyone else in the room is a queen." The gym she went to in the last few years was effectively a gay gym. When the owner, Michael Fenton, offered to stop other members coming in when she was there, she declined. "I like you boys," she said.

❦

"I find it much easier to have a female friendship than a friendship with a man. I am always being followed, which makes it very difficult."

❦

She often asked Palace employees, "Have you any jokes for me?"

❦

"I feel my roots are in Norfolk. I have always loved it there."

❦

She was very well organized: "I do all my Christmas shopping in October."

🌾

Diana told a close friend about her astrologer, Penny Thornton: "Penny was a revelation to me. She made me totally rethink my life. She taught me things about myself I never knew. And her suggestion I should use my own marital difficulties to channel positive ideas into helping others gave me a new direction to my life. That's why I so love my work with Relate [Britain's guidance-counseling service]. I feel I can actually help other people, and that makes me feel so good inside. She has been a godsend."

🌾

"I hate my nose. It's so large. One day I am going to have my conk done."

🌾

There were rumors that she'd had her nose done. Her response: "Honestly, if I had my nose done, do you think I would have chosen this one?"

❦

"I don't like this awful mole above my top lip. I think my legs below the knee are far too thin. I would love a fuller figure, particularly up top."

❦

She told photographer Gemma Levine: "I hate my hands. My hands are awful."

❦

Tom Konig Oppenheimer, a friend from the Earls Court Gym, recalls that his workouts alongside Diana began at 8 A.M., though they went to great lengths never to arrive at the same time, to avoid the relentless attentions of the paparazzi. One morning, Tom and Diana arrived at the same time, and she said, "Oh, my God, now they'll think we're sleeping together!" Having said this, she didn't mind teasing people about the nature of her relationship with Tom. When they ran into each other at a large party, she gave him a huge kiss and said, in front of the entire room, "Oh, Tom, I didn't recognize you with your clothes on!"

❧

While Diana inspected the race car that had won a world championship, journalist Arthur Edwards commented that the police "would never catch you on the M4 motorway in that, ma'am." (She'd been pulled over for speeding a few weeks before.) "I'll tell the jokes, Arthur, thank you," she quipped.

❧

Diana had wanted and gotten a Mercedes 500L, but she decided to give it up. She told Edwards why: "I'm glad I've got rid of it, Arthur. It was like a red beacon, standing out in the traffic. It was nice while I had it, but I don't miss it one bit."

❧

On a funeral floral wreath to her father was a card Diana had personally inscribed: "I miss you dreadfully, Darling Daddy, but will love you forever. . . . Diana."

❦

On the effects of her perceived isolation: "There's no better way to dismantle a personality than to isolate it."

❦

"Wherever you are, come to me," she joked after one of many astrological readings at which a possible suitor was forecast.

❦

"If you find someone you love in life, you must hang on to it."

The Final Days

"I sit in London all the time, and I am abused and followed wherever I go. . . . There is an obsessive interest in me and the children. The constant attention really freaks William out. . . . I was hoping to keep this visit all covered up and quiet. I just want to spend a holiday with my sons, I can't win. What can I do?"

❧

"My sons are always urging me to live abroad and to be less in the public eye. They say it is the only way. Maybe that is what I should do—live abroad."

❧

She took her sons to see the movie *The Devil's Own*, which some feel is sympathetic to the Irish Republican Army. "I didn't know what it was about when I took them. We just wanted to see a movie, and we picked it out of the paper because William likes Harrison Ford. I issued a statement right away, and I called Prince Charles and left a message. I didn't want him to think I was deliberately making trouble."

❦

When asked if she would be seen more often outside London, she replied: "We'll see. I'll have to make sure I don't tread on anyone's toes. William and Harry really enjoy their history lessons because they like learning about their relations."

❦

"My dearest wish is that Charles and I will be able to find a way to do more things together with our sons."

❦

Two months before her death, Diana was asked whether she would ever marry again. "Who would take me on? I have so much baggage. Anyone who takes me out to dinner has to accept the fact that their business will be raked over in the papers.

Photographers will go through their dustbins. I think I am safer alone."

On the increasing speculation that she would marry Dodi al-Fayed, whom she'd been seeing with increasing frequency: "I haven't taken such a long time to get out of one poor marriage to get into another."

Speaking from a motor launch to so-called Rat Pack paparazzi in Saint-Tropez, France: "You are going to get a big surprise. William and Harry have told me to find peace and harmony in my life, and that is what I am going to do. I am going to make an announcement that will shock you all. I am going to make an announcement in two weeks that will put an end to all this. And, boy, will you be surprised."

"It's time I started getting a life. [Dodi] is the man who will take me out of one world into another.

I trust him. I think he can provide everything I need."

❧

"I just love [Dodi's] gentleness, his kindness, and his almost dull way of living. For someone like me, who has lived a goldfish-bowl type of existence, I can't tell you how comforting this is. I like the way he sends flowers. I like the way he conducts himself, not only with me but with women in general."

❧

"Why are the media so anti-Dodi?" she wondered to *Daily Mail* journalist Richard Kay. "Is it because he is a millionaire?"

❧

She would become annoyed when Dodi called and recited a list of presents he had purchased for her. She told her friend Rosa Monckton: "That's not what I want, Rosa. It makes me uneasy. I don't want to be bought. I have everything I want. I just want someone to be there for me, to make me feel safe and secure."

※

"I am very upset at the criticism of him [Dodi]. I've known him for years and we have been close friends for the last five. It was all cleared with Buckingham Palace long ago. It's very difficult for me and the boys to have a private holiday. We couldn't sit in Kensington Palace all summer."

※

"Whatever happens to me in this relationship [with Dodi], I will continue to do my work, and to help where I am needed."

※

While vacationing in Greece with Rosa Monckton just weeks before her death, the paparazzi were particularly relentless. "It's a hunt, Rosa. It's a hunt. Will you really tell people what it is like?"

※

She told Rosa: "I haven't felt as free as this since I was nineteen."

※

In their final telephone conversation, Rosa Monckton asked Diana if she felt blissful in her relationship with Dodi. "Yes, bliss."

※

The day before the crash, Diana told model Cindy Crawford: "For the first time in my life I can say I am truly happy. Dodi is a fantastic man; he fills me with attention and care. I feel once more loved."

※

On the night before she died, on the telephone from Paris, she told Richard Kay: "I do sometimes wonder what's the point. Whatever I do, it's never good enough for some people."

※

She also told Kay: "I'm coming home tomorrow and the boys will be back from Scotland in the evening. I will have a few days with them before they're back at school."

✾

About the lunar eclipse (which happened the day after she died), Diana told her personal astrologer: "That's the day I get my boys back."

✾

Her last words to Richard Kay: "Unplug your phone and get a good night's sleep."

✾

She was once asked whether she gambled. "Not with cards," she replied, "but with life."

✾

She once wondered out loud to a royal milliner, "If anything ever happens to me, Mr. Sommerville, do you think they'll think of me as another Jackie Kennedy?"

Diana's tribute

"I can honestly say that one of my greatest pleasures has been my association with people.... I've been allowed to share your thoughts and dreams, your disappointments, and your happiness. You have also given me an education by teaching me more about life and living than any books or teachers could have done. My debt of gratitude to you all is immense. I hope in some small way I have been of service in return. Your kindness and affection have carried me through some of the most difficult periods, and always your love and care have eased that journey. And for that, I thank you from the bottom of my heart."